EVENTING EXPLAINED

EVENTING
EXPLAINED

Liza Randall

Published in association with British Eventing

**BRITISH
EVENTING**

Providing the ultimate
equestrian challenge

Kenilworth Press

First published in the UK in 2012
by Kenilworth Press, an imprint of Quiller Publishing Ltd

British Library Cataloguing-in-Publication Data
A catalogue record for this book is available from the British Library

ISBN 978 1 905693 47 3

Design and typesetting by Paul Saunders
Printed in China

Kenilworth Press
An imprint of Quiller Publishing Ltd
Wykey House, Wykey, Shrewsbury, SY4 1JA
Tel: 01939 261616 Fax: 01939 261606
E-mail: info@quillerbooks.com
Website: www.kenilworthpress.co.uk

CONTENTS

ACKNOWLEDGEMENTS

This book would have not been possible without the generous help of the many experts and contributors, all involved in the wonderful sport of eventing, who are listed below, so thank you all.

Also, special thanks to my mum, Moira and my husband Karl for looking after toddler Tom when I was writing!

Photography and imagery

Adam Fanthorpe, expert event photographer, www.fanthorpes.co.uk

Dianne Breeze, dressage rider, trainer and ace cartoonist

Liza Randall, Michelle Scammel, Karl Randall and Claire Johnson

Simon Lusty, pilates photographs

Contributors

British Eventing, www.britisheventing.com

Course Designer and Event Organiser, Janet Plant, Hartpury College
Course Designer and British Eventing CEO, Mike Etherington-Smith
Course Designer and Technical Assistant, Adrian Ditcham

Dentistry, Gemma Lilly, The Donkey Trust
British Association of Equine Dental Technicians, www.baedt.com

Horse Fitness, Kathryn Nankevis, The Equine Therapy Centre, Hartpury College

Grooming, Liz Daniels and Jodie Summers

The British Grooms Association, www.britishgrooms.org.uk

Farriery, Haydn Price, Olympic Team farrier, and farrier John Chilman

Hat and Body Protectors, BETA, www.beta-uk.org

Horse Nutrition, Dr Teresa Hollands, Dodson and Horrell, www.dodsonandhorrell.com

Lorinery, Peter Lusty and Tricia Nassau-Williams, The Worshipful Company of Loriners, www.lorinery.co.uk

Physiotherapy Rachel Greetham, www.equineandcaninesolutions.co.uk www.acpat.org.uk

Pilates, Liza Randall, www.panaceapilates.co.uk

Rider Nutrition, Julia Scott Douglas

Saddlery, Worshipful Company of Master Saddlers, www.saddlersco.co.uk

Sports Psychology, Nikki Heath, www.symbioticsltd.com

Veterinary, Liz Brown, Partner at Lambourn Equine Vets, British Eventing Senior Team Vet

British Equine Veterinary Association, www.beva.org.uk

World Class, British Equestrian Federation, www.bef.org.uk

BE Accredited coaches and event riders and trainers

(See www.britisheventing.com for contact details)

Yogi Breisner, British Eventing Performance Director

Peter Murphy, British Eventing Showjump Coach

Georgie Barnes	Lizzie Murray
Laura Bechtolsheimer	Janet Plant
Geoff Billington	Sue Ringrose
John Bowen	Louise Smales
Muriel Colquhoun, MBE	Sue Stewart
Deborah Fielding	Millie Tonks
Lucinda Green	Oliver Townend
Mandy Holloway	Jane Wallace
Kate Johnston	Gemma Wood
Warren Lamperd	

FOREWORD

YOGI BREISNER

World Class Performance Manager and Chef d'Equipe
to the British Eventing team

Eventing is possibly the most exciting of all equestrian disciplines. It combines the grace and testing of correct training in the dressage phase with the precision and accuracy of the showjumping element, and the excitement, courage and flair of cross country riding. Being an all-round sport the participants also need an all-round training schedule which covers not just the horse's training but the rider's too. This training should be based on the classical equestrian methods of working the horse in a balanced, rhythmical and forward way whereby control is achieved through willing obedience. Eventing is not only a test of the participant's training and riding skills but also of their horse care, management and horsemanship. This book is the start to achieving all this.

Best of luck!

Yogi

YOGI BREISNER

INTRODUCTION TO BRITISH EVENTING

British Eventing (BE) is the National Governing Body of the growing sport of eventing in Great Britain. There's a 'ladder of progression' through the sport with levels beginning at the popular BE80(T) (80cm high fences) leading to BE90 and BE100 right through to the highest level (advanced) with fences up to 1.20m. Events are spread around the country, catering for over 75,000 starters.

There are annual championships as well as regional competitions, and BE aims to cater for all levels of horse and competitor when and wherever you want to ride. Successful BE90 and BE100 riders can find themselves competing at the British Eventing Grassroots Championship held at Badminton.

BE prides itself on the standards of its events. All affiliated events have to comply with the highest possible standards of safety, efficiency and course presentation, and all events are stewarded by a BE steward and a BE technical adviser to ensure compliance with the rules and regulations and expected standards. Most events are run on land owned by individuals or estates.

BE has a readily available list of recognised officials (stewards, technical advisers and scorers), course designers and builders, and accredited coaches. Details on all training activities and competition opportunities can be found on the website, www.britisheventing.com, and can be booked online.

The easiest place to find out more about the sport is to log on to the BE website or to call the BE office on 02476 698856, where the team will be very

OPPOSITE The exhilaration is evident after completing the three phases.

British Eventing courses are built to the highest standards.

happy to share further information about the sport, how to join BE, how to acquire day tickets and how to get started. It is not as intimidating as you might think, as more than 11,000 members can testify to.

It is a great sport; Team GB has fantastic success on the world stage, the events are well organised and delivered, and there is something for everyone – give us a call and come and try!

MIKE ETHERINGTON-SMITH

Course Designer and CEO, British Eventing

WELCOME!

You've chosen to be a part of a really exciting sport! So whether you're an adult or a teenager wanting to try eventing for the first time, or a parent or helper, read on! In the following pages you'll discover how you can start eventing at a level that's right for you, and find professional training from BE accredited coaches.

Eventing is a very well-established sport in the UK, offering riders a continuous stream of competitions during the season. There was a time when eventing stopped during the summer, but because of mobile ground-care equipment, advances in course design and attention paid to creating good going whatever the weather, the eventing calendar has grown to what it is today.

The calendar boasts over 300 competition days, with everything from BE80(T) to Advanced sections held midweek and every weekend from March through to October. A myriad of organisers run these events, located everywhere from the low rolling hills of Somerset right up to the picturesque parkland of Moray in North-east Scotland.

In this book, as well as looking in detail at how to get started, you can read about how an event runs, look up training tips, and see the fences you may meet across country. You'll also find out what equipment you need, which is probably far less than you may have thought!

Eventing Explained also looks at how courses have developed over the years, and delves into aspects of horse and rider welfare that will enhance your overall eventing experience. Rider sections include sports psychology, fitness and eating plans, and there are sections on farriery, equine dentistry and world-class turnout tips for your horse.

Eventing Explained has taken advice from a number of eventing experts who all lead in their chosen field, including Olympic riders, trainers, vets and top equestrian professionals. So sit back, relax and let your eventing experience begin.

The author enjoying a BE100 event in Cheshire.

1

WHAT IS EVENTING?

Here you'll find details on the different levels you can try in affiliated eventing and how to get started.

If you like a bit of everything, then eventing is for you! It combines all the great skills of horsemanship and is often described as the equestrian equivalent of a triathlon. The three phases are scored individually, and then these scores are added together following the final phase to give a total score. In one-day events you'll do dressage first, followed by showjumping and cross country. As you move up the levels, or take part in international competitions, like a Novice 1★ event, the whole format changes, with the competition spread over three days. You'll need to get your best gear on for the trot up, then dressage, cross country and finally showjumping. Eventing is also the only sport where you'll very often find yourself competing against professional riders and even Olympic stars as they bring their young horses through the levels.

You may find yourself competing in the same section as one of your eventing heroes!

Entry level eventing

Whether you're 11 or 60, if you are at home jumping small fences, enjoy a bit of flatwork and would like to bring it all together, then you'll love affiliated eventing. Ponies as well as horses can compete, as long as they're at least five years old (four if competing in a dedicated Young Horse class or BE80(T)) and are at least 142cm in height.

All affiliated events are run under national guidelines, have extremely high standards of fence construction and adhere to strict safety rules that regulate medical, veterinary and competition standards for every phase.

The table opposite offers an analysis of the key elements involved in the basic levels of the sport.

Enjoying the canter to the finish timers.

Key elements

Phases	BE80(T)	BE90	BE100	BE100 Plus
Dressage • In a 20 x 40m or 20 x 60m arena (mostly grass) • Similar in standard to British Dressage Prelim & Novice • Results shown as penalty points	British Eventing dressage tests	British Eventing dressage tests	British Eventing dressage tests	British Eventing dressage tests
Showjumping • Inviting, flowing courses with plenty of room, with a double combination	• 7–12 numbered obstacles • Two obstacles at a maximum height of 0.85m, the rest at 0.80m • 325mpm speed	• 8–12 numbered obstacles • Two obstacles at a maximum height of 0.95m, the rest at 0.90m • 325mpm speed	• 8–12 numbered obstacles • Two obstacles at a maximum height of 1.05m, the rest at 1.00m • 325mpm speed • At least one double combination	• 8–12 numbered obstacles • Two obstacles at a maximum height of 1.10m, the rest at 1.05m • 325mpm speed • At least one double combination
Cross Country • Courses may include uphill and downhill fences, small drops, banks, ditches, water, spreads and ascending fences. • Some combinations will have less demanding alternatives.	• 18–25 jumping efforts • 1,600–2,800m course • 435mpm speed • Max height 0.80m • Max spread (top) 0.90m • Max spread (base) 1.25m • Open to Grade 4 horses and ponies only, day ticket horses and ponies without points • There is no obligation to move out of BE80(T) • No points will be awarded	• 18–25 jumping efforts • 1,600–2,800m course • 450mpm speed • Max height 0.90m • Max spread (top) 1.00m • Max spread (base) 1.50m • Open to Grade 4 horses and ponies only, day ticket horses and ponies without points • There is no obligation to move out of BE90 • Foundation points are awarded	• 18–25 jumping efforts • 1,600–2,800m course • 475mpm speed • Max height 1.00m • Max spread (top) 1.10m • Max spread (base) 1.80m • Open to Grade 4 horses and ponies without points that are either registered or have day tickets • There is no obligation to move out of BE100 • Foundation points are awarded	• 18–25 jumping efforts • 1,600–2,800m course • 475mpm speed • Max height 1.00m • Max spread (top) 1.10m • Max spread (base) 1.80m • Open to Grade 4 horses and ponies without points that are either registered or have day tickets • There is no obligation to move out of BE100 • Foundation points are awarded

More about the levels

BE80(T) training class

This is a training class aimed at new riders or new horse and rider combinations. You can either treat it as the first step on your way through the levels, or you can stay at BE80(T). However, if your horse is experienced and has points at Novice level you'll need to run non-competitively (HC).

The cross country fences will be no higher than 80cm with one or two showjumps at a maximum height of 85cm, while the rest are 80cm or lower.

Ponies are welcome at affliated events so long as they are at least 142cm.

This is a fantastic class for you to gain experience and confidence as it is held under the watchful eye of a BE accredited coach (see page 137). If you wish, the coach can help you to warm up for each phase and will also take you on an instructional walk of the cross country and showjumping courses. You'll find their details, plus the times of the course-walks, displayed in the secretary's tent on the day of your event. Their help is optional, and included in the cost of your entry fee.

Before you enter a BE80(T), make sure you've done some training and feel capable enough to canter around the course in a good rhythm. You'll be expected to go up and down slopes, and jump a variety of straightforward fences (see the section on page 137). The course will be inviting, flowing, balanced and encouraging, with the minimum amount of technicality involved so both you and your horse will grow in confidence while having fun.

Time is not a key element at BE80(T) level, but have a look at the Key Elements table on page 21 for a précis on what's involved in each phase.

You'll find the dressage tests in your BE *Members' Handbook* or on the BE website at www.britisheventing.com

BE90

If you already have some experience, then perhaps BE90 or BE100 may be the class for you.

At BE90 the fences are higher and wider than for BE80(T), but are still built to encourage a flowing round, whether in the showjumping or cross country phases. Time on the cross country is still generous at 450mpm. Have a look at the Ket Elements table on page 21 for details.

You won't have the advantage of an accredited coach, so remember to leave plenty of time for your preparation, such as course-walking and warming up.

If your horse has BE points, you can compete in a BE90 Open class. You can also start to collect foundation points for double clear rounds and if you and your horse are placed.

Pick your class according to your and your horse's experience.

BE100

At BE100 the challenge intensifies as classes increase in technicality and height, and the talents and experience of horse and rider are put to the test. Again the heights and spreads of the fences change, with a maximum showjumping height of 1.05m and a maximum height in the cross country of 1m. The cross country fence spreads are wider, with a maximum base spread of 1.80m.

At BE100, time on the cross country begins to become a factor in the context of the competition, as the optimum time is based on 475mpm.

The course will be inviting and flowing and is designed so that it is consistent and demanding enough that if you are successful at this level, you could progress to Novice with confidence, yet inviting enough to allow you to remain at BE100 if that is where you feel comfortable.

At this level you should feel confident jumping the course in a rhythm over a variety of straightforward fences including going up and down slopes and across undulations.

See the Key Elements table on page 21 for more details.

You can also collect foundation points at BE100 as points are awarded for double clear rounds and if you and your horse are placed.

Involving the whole family!

BE100 Plus

If you're looking for an extra challenge but don't yet want to step up to Novice, then BE100 Plus is right for you. The dressage tests remain as at BE100 and so does the cross country, but the showjumping course is a little more technical, with a maximum height of 1.10m.

Open classes

Open classes at BE90 and BE100 are intended for riders and horses that have experience, or horses that have accumulated points at Novice and beyond. Generally, the entry level classes are open to horses without points, known as Grade 4 horses. Riders are excluded from riding competitively in certain classes if they have recently competed at Advanced level or above. Horses with points, and riders who have competed at a high level, will need to ride hors concours in such a class, or else enter the Open section. Check the BE website or *Members' Handbook* for more details.

BE100 three-day events

If you want to experience how it would feel to compete over three days like the top eventers at Badminton or Burghley, then you could plan to work towards doing a BE100 three-day event. Perhaps have it as a goal at the end of your second season.

To compete in a three-day event your horse must be a Grade 4 horse and at least six years old. You must have completed three clear rounds cross country with no more than 16 showjumping faults in all, excluding time penalties, in BE100 or above. There are a few more rules that you need to keep in mind as they are based on the FEI rules, so it is always important to check the BE website.

If your horse has points at Novice level, some events also run Open classes for which he may be eligible.

If your horse has BE points, you can compete in an Open class.

Members' Handbook

An essential A5 guide for all eventers! It's colour-coded and arranged in six sections of Membership, Horses and Classification; Entries and Withdrawals; Regulations for the Conduct of Events; Regulations for the Individual Tests; International Events and Disciplinary Regulations.

The rest of the Handbook is divided into Annexes which cover subjects like permitted saddlery and equipment, competitors' dress rules, championships, faults and current eventing dressage tests.

It also has a full list of contact details for all BE officials and organisers, plus an invaluable list of accredited coaches all over the UK who are happy to help you succeed in eventing. You'll also find the *Members' Handbook* online at www.britisheventing.com

Youth programmes

British Eventing operates various youth programmes. Log on to www.britisheventing.com/youtheventing to find out the latest news.

There are great opportunities for youngsters to compete in affiliated eventing.

2

COMPETING
WITH BRITISH EVENTING

British Eventing (BE) is the governing body for the sport of eventing in the United Kingdom, and is the hub of membership and entry activity.

All affiliated events must run their competitions in line with BE's Rules, which means everything from competition levels, medical provisions, ground conditions, fence materials and types are regulated and monitored before and during the competition. Also the verified scores at an event are

Spectators enjoying a day out.

entered directly onto BE's database by a BE-trained scorer so a complete and accurate record is kept of every round you do!

BE's involvement doesn't stop there as, following an event, they receive reports from various officials including the technical adviser (TA), steward and event doctor. For example, the TA will record how each and every fence jumped in the cross country, noting whether there were any particular issues. This data can then be analysed at a touch of a button, so trends are easily recognised as regards fence types and styles. This information is then shared with course designers and builders to make improvements.

Registration and membership

To take part in BE competitions, you'll need to register yourself and your horse, which is easy to do online at www.britisheventing.com, or you can do it by post. Registration is compulsory for any type of membership you wish to take out. BE will also need to see a copy of your horse's name page and breeding details from his passport, which you can send in after you've registered. Make sure that your registration and membership are sorted for yourself and your horse a couple of months in advance of your first competition. Entries are taken well in advance and if you and your horse are not registered, you cannot enter.

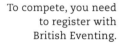

To compete, you need to register with British Eventing.

Membership options

In order to start competing you have three membership options to choose from, which are a day ticket, training ticket (BE80(T) only) or full membership. Just remember that you need to buy membership for both yourself and your horse, unless you are buying training tickets, in which case membership for yourself and your horse is combined.

Training tickets

You don't need to be a full member to have a go at BE80(T). Training tickets for a BE80(T) class can be bought in the same way as a day ticket for BE90 or BE100. This way you can enjoy a taste of affiliated eventing before you take out full membership for yourself and a season ticket for your horse.

Training tickets are a combined horse and rider ticket and you can purchase an unlimited amount in a season. A training ticket gives you the same benefits as a day ticket, such as day membership and insurance. See the BE website for details.

It's also a good idea to buy *British Eventing Life*, BE's bi-monthly magazine which carries all the event schedules.

A much-loved family pony enjoying the Grassroot Championships at Badminton.

Day tickets

If you want to ride at BE90, BE100 up to Intermediate Novice, you can compete on a day ticket. Remember you'll need to buy a day ticket for both yourself and for your horse.

You can buy day tickets from the BE website or by post before making an entry to the event of your choice. You can buy as many day tickets as you like for your *horse*, but *you* are limited to only four per year.

For peace of mind, day tickets include public liability and personal accident insurance for the period of the event (check website for details), so you don't need to arrange cover separately. As soon as you buy your first day ticket, you'll will be sent the BE *Members' Handbook*, which carries all the dressage test information you'll need, as well as all the current rules and regulations for the class you are entering.

Eventing is enjoyed by riders of all ages and abilities.

Full membership

Let's assume that you have now caught the eventing bug after competing on day tickets and want to take the next step. That would be full membership for you and a season ticket for your horse. As a full member and season ticket holder you will have unlimited competition opportunities and exclusive members' benefits as well as preferential entries. (Alternatively, you can purchase a half season ticket.)

When you buy a season ticket online you'll be given your horse's ballot numbers and relevant month for the whole season. (Otherwise you will be posted a set of ballot stickers detailing a month and number). One of these can be used during each of the ballot periods (as shown in the Event Schedule). These allow you to have entry priority at one event of your choice during that period. You'll also get two super ballot numbers that you can use to give you extra priority if there is an event that you *really* want to get into.

VETERINARY TIPS **Vaccinations**

Your horse will need to be up-to-date with his vaccinations, so ensure that he's had a primary course of two injections against equine influenza, no less than 21 days, and no more than 92 days, apart. Once he's had these first two injections he can compete.

In addition, a first booster injection must be given no less than 150 days and no more than 215 days after the second injection of the primary course. Subsequently, booster injections must be given at intervals of no more than one year apart. None of these injections must have been given within the seven days preceding a competition.

Grading of horses

To ensure fair competition, horses are graded according to the number of BE points they have gained from being placed (if any). Grading points are not awarded at BE80(T), but at BE90 and BE100 your horse can accumulate foundation points (FP) that are awarded for double clear rounds. You can look up a horse's competition record on the British Eventing website, where all points, including notional foundation points, are listed.

No points/foundation points	Grade 4
1–20 points	Grade 3
21–60 points	Grade 2
61+ points	Grade 1

Entering an event

Choosing where to compete

As events are run by varying organisers and held at different venues, which competitions you decide to go to is entirely your choice. But it may be useful to take into account:

- your trainer's advice

- distance from your yard

- location and type of course, e.g. hilly, flat, etc.

- fitness of horse/rider.

If you're lucky enough to live close to an Eventing Centre that runs a few competitions a year, have a dry run before you enter (see page 37) so you know exactly what to expect, especially if you haven't been to an affiliated event before.

Making an entry

You can enter most competitions online at www.britisheventing.com or the BDWP website at www.bdwp.co.uk

It's important to read all the details in the online or magazine schedule as it has been condensed for easy reading!

Each event will state which entry system it's using. For postal entries, send your entry with a self-seal stamped addressed envelope with a cheque to the entries secretary's address (not the organiser), or as detailed in the schedule. Remember to send in your entry well before the ballot date (see page 35) and remember that oversubscribed events will ballot on that date, which is well before the closing date for entries.

In the magazine the schedules are all set out in the same format. It's been designed to convey at a glance when entries open and close and to give ballot information, details of the classes and fees. It gives details of what levels of classes are running (e.g. BE80(T), BE90), the days of the week, dressage test information, start fee and total payable. It also lists the entry fee, abandonment premium and late entry surcharge fee. If you enter before the late entry surcharge date, the amount you pay is shown in the total payable column,

ABOVE Badminton House.

Preparation is the key to competing at any event.

which includes the abandonment premium (this is the insurance you pay per *class* – not per *day* – that covers your entry fee if the event has to be cancelled for any reason.

The start fee is also listed; this is what the organiser uses to pay for reinvestment into the course, and also goes towards the medical costs for the event. Each event has on average two or three event doctors, two paramedics, two land ambulances, two event vets and a horse ambulance. Quite a commitment to you and your horse's safety!

After the close of entries, you'll receive an email or postal confirmation of your entry, number and section. Check these details are correct, note any special information and keep it in a safe place, as you'll need the information when you either check online or phone for your start times.

Each affiliated event has an average of two to three doctors, two paramedics, two land ambulances, two vets and a horse ambulance. Quite a commitment to your and your horse's safety.

Points relating to entry

Hopefully, your entry will be accepted, everything will run smoothly on the lead-up to the event, and you will go ahead as intended. However, it's useful to know how to proceed if things don't go quite to plan.

Withdrawing

Once you've entered you're expected to compete unless you need to withdraw for some reason. If you withdraw before the ballot date you'll receive a full refund. The situation regarding withdrawal after the ballot date can vary, so check the refund policy in the schedule. Also check out the Withdrawals Rule in the BE *Members' Handbook*.

Balloting

A number of events are really popular and are oversubscribed in many classes, so it's wise to use your ballot number or sticker if you're a full member. If you're balloted out after using a ballot number, you'll have an assured entry to your next event as you'll be given a super priority entry number to use for your next competition.

First to start in the early morning mist.

Day ticket entries have no priority in the event of a ballot, except that full BE members with day ticket horses will take precedence over other day ticket entries. If you are balloted out or have to withdraw prior to the published ballot date, your entry will be refunded.

Wait lists

Some oversubscribed events may set up a wait list, details of which you will find in the event's schedule.

3

PREPARATION AND TRAINING

Preparation is key when you want to event. Not only must you be ready for the big day, but your preparation must start months back with the essential training you need to tackle the three phases successfully, and the fitness work needed for both you and your horse.

The dry run

Ideally, take a day to visit an affiliated event (without your equine friend!), to see what it's like and how it runs. Take along your parents, other half or helper so that they can also have a good look around and know what to expect. It's important to visit the same level of competition you're going to enter, so you'll get a good idea of how it works, see the height of the fences, walk a similar cross country course and watch what goes on in the collecting rings.

It helps to do your 'on the ground' research in a logical manner – looking at the three phases in the same way as how you will on your competition day, so your helpers will know what is going on and what happens next – it leads to less 'headless chicken' activity on the actual day of your competition!

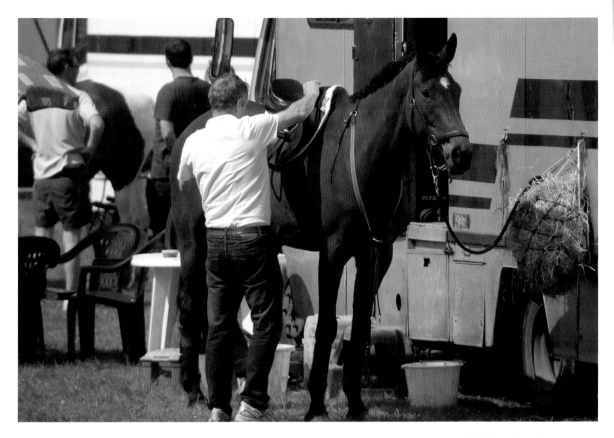

A helper at work.

The horsebox park

Start off by having a look around the horsebox park; if you have previously competed in a couple of Riding Club or Pony Club events, you may find that the park seems very packed and busy, with riders and their grooms getting ready for each phase of the competition.

Remember, for many people, eventing is their day job, so they are taking along a lorryload of horses to compete so that they can move them through the levels. So don't be surprised if you get to park alongside an Olympic champion! They all have to give their young horses experience.

The secretary's tent

Next, go along to the secretary's tent. Here riders register, pay their start fees, get their hats tagged and collect their numbers (two sheets, one for the front and one for the back of the bib) and programme. Here you'll also find the

OPPOSITE Moral support on the way to the start box.

scoreboards detailing the sections, and the rider representative details. If you're going to compete in a BE80(T) section, the secretary will also be able to tell you the times of the showjumping and cross country course-walk, or you'll see the information pinned on a notice board in the tent. You can also view the cross country course plan and find out the optimum time for the cross country phase.

Hat tagging

You can't compete in any BE jumping phase without your hat harness visibly displaying a BE tag. This shows the steward that your hat meets the be safety rules. Before your first event, check the BE website for relevant standards, as you may need to buy a new hat if you have had yours a while.

At your first event, or the day before if you are walking the course, take your hat to the secretary, who will check that it is labelled with the appropriate BETA or international safety standard relevant to eventing. Following this compliance check, the secretary will put a loop of yellow sticky tape bearing the BE logo on your hat harness.

All hats that pass the safety check on site are marked with a yellow tag on the hat's harness.

When walking around the trade stand area, you'll notice that there are no horses around the outside of the arenas, and that's because the organisers take care to keep horses away from the public for safety. At many events, horse-walks are set up to get competitors safely from one phase to the next and back to the horsebox park. These are usually made up of a series of ropes, so when you're competing, make sure you make a note of where the horse-walks are for each phase.

The dressage area

When you get to the dressage area, you'll notice two or more arenas marked up, with gaps between and around them for riders to work-in when they're called forward at their allotted time for the test by the collecting ring steward. In front of the arenas, you'll see a marked-off area for general working-in. Here, also, will be volunteer stewards with clipboards that list the dressage times of each competitor for each section. Observe the working-in arena and

Working-in areas should be clearly marked.

the work of the stewards so you can see how this phase runs, then watch a few tests. You'll see some riders carrying a whip and with boots on their horse while in the warm-up area, which is permitted. But they'll need to remove them before going into the test arena. Try to see the exact test that you'll be performing on your big day, so you can see the pattern of it in the arena and ride the test in your mind. When you're happy, take your helpers up to the showjumping arena.

Remember to remove your horse's boots before going into the arena.

The showjumping arena

For the showjumping, competitors need to declare their entry to the collecting ring steward who's running the ring as soon as they arrive there. The steward will mark off their number on a blackboard or clipboard and give an idea of timings. This is something your helpers can do for you on the day, leaving you to focus on your warm-up.

Observe a few riders warming up – perhaps watch a couple of the professionals and their grooms, so your helpers can see what their role will be in the arena and how they can help you by setting up practice fences on the day.

There are always two, and sometimes three, practice fences in every showjumping warm-up arena at an affiliated event. One is set up as a cross-pole, which can then be changed to an upright; the other is set up as a small oxer. It's important that the height of the practice fences should reflect the height of the fences in the ring so, for example, they should be no higher than 95cm if you are competing in the BE90 class. Even so, start with a small cross-pole then gradually raise the height as appropriate for your class.

To help avoid crashes in the collecting rings, the practice fences must be jumped with the red flag or marker, which is attached to the wing, to your right.

You'll notice that the professional riders do not jump continuously over the practice fences for the ten minutes or so before their time. They only jump about four or five fences because they're conserving their own and their horse's energy and strength for the phases ahead.

A rider is usually called forward by the steward to enter the arena once the previous competitor is riding their last line of fences. Once in, the steward

The steward has marked down the running order. It is important to check in with them on arrival.

Enjoy your round!

will close the ropes behind the competitor and they'll start their round *once the bell has gone*, making sure to pass through the starting timers positioned a couple of metres in front of the first fence.

The cross country course

Again, first make your way to the practice area. You'll see that riders don't spend too much time in the warm-up area before their round, as they've already hacked for five minutes or so to get to the start of the course and they'll want to conserve their horse's energy for the cross country ahead. Of course, the precise routine you decide upon will depend on your own and your horse's experience and the timetable you are working to on the day. For example, if you have just showjumped, changed your tack and hacked down to the start then you'll do less than if your showjumping was three hours earlier.

If the event is running one or two class levels that day, you'll see a few different practice fences of various heights, distinguished by their colour numbers: purple for BE80(T), orange for BE90, pink for BE100.

Ready for the off.

The starter will call forward the rider who is next to start and will give them a countdown, for example 'two minutes' … 'one minute' … 'thirty seconds' … It's up to the rider at what count they enter the start box and whether they have assistance from their helpers to hold the horse. Usually if a horse is quiet, a rider will enter the start box on the fifteen or ten seconds count and wait, but if a horse is very eager to go, it may be better to walk into the box on five seconds. Following the signal to go, or when the horse's nose crosses the start line – whichever is the earlier – the timer will start. It will stop once the horse's nose passes the finish line. A rider who deliberately leaves the start box during the countdown before the starter says go, may be eliminated. (The word 'may' is used here because, in some circumstances, a dis-cretionary lesser penalty may be applied, but best advice is to make sure you avoid doing this!)

The starter will count you down.

On the course

Once a competitor has started, their progress around the course is monitored by the fence judges, who relay the competitor's progress to the controller and commentator, who are assisted by their team of stewards, collectively known as control. This, like the scorer's office, is probably the busiest place you will find at an event, as it takes a great deal of skill to multi-task when things are happening literally at the galloping! (See the chapter Who's Who at Affiliated Events for more details.)

Control – one of the busiest places on an eventing cross country course.

British Eventing training

British Eventing have an easy-to-use section of the website where you can book in at local training clinics and camps at the right level for you – just visit www.britisheventing.com/training to book online.

4

HORSE FITNESS

A good fitness programme is a vital part of your preparation. Here we look at interval training, canter work, assessing speed and looking after your horse's health.

Fittening your horse

When bringing your horse into work remember that the slow work (walking exercise) is essential to condition muscles and harden tendons. Fast work (canters) shouldn't be started until the horse is basically fit and even then should start relatively slow and gradually increase in time, either with a suitable interval or cross-training programme as advised by your coach, or through a steady progression of work.

If you want to increase fitness, carry out a progressively increasing programme of work. For a horse already in regular work, increase the frequency, duration and intensity of work each week, no more than six weeks away from the competition (less for an athletic, Thoroughbred type). Repeating the same work pattern week after week will not increase fitness.

Canter work

Incorporate one 'canter day' per week, when you practise your fast work, after either hacking or boxing to a suitable field or gallop. These canters can be achieved in a number of ways, for example cross country schooling days

will count as 'canter day'. Canter work up hills is great but don't forget to practise riding downhill and across slopes as well. Horses need to learn how to shift their balance to their hindquarters when going downhill, so don't neglect this part of your training. In the eventing off-season, hunting is an excellent way to develop your horse's balance and coordination across variable terrain, and will also improve your own balance and endurance in the saddle. You will find the nearest Drag or Hunt Kennels listed in the telephone book or online.

Assessing your speed

Learn to assess the speed of your horse's cross country canter. Mark out a distance and time yourself over it. Speed is distance divided by time.

Speeds and jumping efforts at basic level

BE80(T)	BE90	BE100
18–25 jumping efforts	18–25 jumping efforts	18–25 jumping efforts
1,600–2,800m course	1,600–2,800m course	1,600–2,800m course
Speed 435mpm	Speed 450mpm	Speed 475mpm

At an event, the optimum time for each cross country course is displayed in the secretary's tent and at the start box. It's worked out by the technical adviser (TA) who measures the length of the course accurately from start to finish, using a measuring wheel or satellite device, passing between all the flags and across the fences as a horse would. This accurate distance is then converted to an optimum time by dividing it by the metres per minute allowed at each level.

Make sure you carry out some of your canter work at a speed 10 per cent above that of the speed needed to make your optimum time. You don't need to maintain this for more than a kilometre at most, but doing so will help prepare your horse for the extra effort involved in negotiating the fences within the optimum time. Quality is more important than quantity and it is more beneficial to carrying out one good canter session per week than to be clocking up miles of hacking in walk and trot.)

OPPOSITE Remember to praise your horse when he has done well.

Assessing fitness

If it is your first time eventing, assess your horse's fitness one month before the competition by cantering a distance (or duration) similar to that of the course, but without the fences.

If you have a Thoroughbred, or predominantly Thoroughbred horse, you may not need any more specific fitness than this type of cross-training; there is nothing to be gained by having a horse far fitter than he needs to be. A horse that is too strong and pulling against you will actually use more energy than a horse that goes in a steady rhythm.

Variety is important for physical and mental wellbeing. Incorporate as many types of work as possible, so make sure you have schooled and ridden dressage tests on grass as well as on an artificial surface, and include some grass or field schooling in your weekly programme. When training in an arena, pay as much attention to the surface you school on as the surfaces you gallop and jump on. Avoid deep, boggy and patchy arena surfaces for schooling.

For both your sakes, don't be afraid to give your horse a day off each week. A horse that is out at grass for most of the day will have a better baseline fitness than a stable-kept horse.

Health during fittening

Keep a keen and critical eye on your horse's foot balance and shoeing cycle; if he has a good platform to work from, he'll be more efficient over the ground and less likely to incur injury along the way. Horses with long toes and low heels are more likely to have time off with bruised feet and or tendon or ligament injury.

If you have any concerns about your horse's weight, energy levels or soundness, consult your vet before embarking on an increasing work programme. If your horse has some underlying health issues, increasing his workload could be counterproductive. If you encounter setbacks during the course of your preparation, try not to worry too much; horses lose fitness more slowly than humans. If your horse has been in regular work, going out most days, schooling, hacking and jumping, he can afford to lose up to two weeks in the run-up to the competition without a significant loss of fitness. Always aim to take a healthy, sound horse to a competition rather than asking a lame horse to carry on regardless. Horses seen to be lame at an event will be immediately eliminated and referred to the event vet.

Try not to 'over-prepare' at the eleventh hour by cramming in lessons and schooling sessions in the final week. Aim to get any of this final preparation out of the way three days beforehand to ensure that your horse arrives refreshed and ready to go at the competition.

Your horse should be fit for the rigours of the cross country as terrain will vary.

Remember to take water and buckets when you train away from home so you can wash your horse down afterwards.

VETERINARY TIPS Banned substances

Competitors at all levels should be familiar with the drug regulations that apply to all competitions run under BE or FEI rules. Your horse may be drug tested at any competition so it is important not to get caught out. The regulations are on the BE and FEI websites and individual substances can be checked on www.feicleansport.org. Prohibited substances are classified as 'banned' (those which should never be used in a competition horse), or 'controlled medication' (substances which have a therapeutic role but need to be out of the system before the horse competes). Controlled medication substances have a withdrawal period; you should ask your vet about

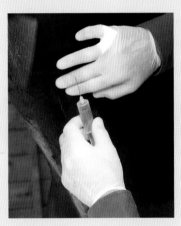

Vet taking a blood sample.

these and also inform the vet about any competitions you have entered before any treatments are given.

There are several circumstances that can lead to a positive test for the unsuspecting rider. For example, ACP given to aid clipping can take two weeks to get out of a horse's system. Procaine penicillin has a prolonged withdrawal period and should be avoided, as most other antibiotics have no withdrawal time. Some skin creams contain corticosteroids or other prohibited substances.

Cross contamination is also common, especially through feed buckets. It's essential that, if a horse on the yard needs medication, he must have a separate mixing spoon and bucket – perhaps colour-coded – which is only used for that medication, and the medication should be added immediately prior to feeding.

Some feeds, supplements and products that are readily available contain banned substances. Don't be fooled by thinking that herbal-based products are safe – this is not always the case. Anything that your horse consumes, comes into contact with, or has applied to him should be checked.

Feeding the event horse

Although it is something that we tend to take for granted, without proper nutrition, your horse's full potential will not be realised. Nutrition supports peak performance, sustains training levels, helps recovery from injury and reduces the horse's susceptibility to injury and infection. (The same applies to you, the rider – see Nutrition, page 87.)

Moving from unaffiliated eventing to affiliated means that you'll need to feed for the extra demands for performance, as well as providing your horse with nutritional support for his general health and welfare; but it doesn't need to be complicated.

Regardless of the level of work or the nature of your horse, whether he's a Warmblood or a Thoroughbred, what you feed your horse has three main roles: for bulk, energy and health.

Bulk

You need to provide enough bulk to meet his physiological and psychological need to chew. This is achieved by feeding a minimum of 1.5 per cent of his bodyweight per day as fibre so that his digestive system stays healthy and he can eat 16–18 hours out of 24.

Bulk needs to be fed at 1.5 per cent of your horse's bodyweight per day.

Research shows that maintaining fibre intake decreases the risks of colic, gastric ulcers and the development of stereotypical behaviour (wind-sucking, crib-biting, etc.) and is therefore essential for your horse's welfare and performance. Fibre can provide calories as well as being a filler, so pick the right type for your horse.

TOP TIPS Practical feeding

- Giving ad lib fibre should mean that there is some forage left in the stable in the morning. However, play with the quantities if you have too much left. If you give *too little* forage, your horse could finish after a couple of hours and be left with nothing for the remainder of the night, which is bad for him psychologically and physically can be a cause of gastric ulcers.

- The forages, hay and haylage, are the most commonly recognised sources of fibre. However fibre can be provided by grass, sugar-beet, chaffs, high-fibre cubes and the outer husks of cereals (40 per cent of human fibre is provided by whole grains!).

- All hay for performance horses should be soaked for a minimum of half an hour prior to feeding to dampen any dust. All hay (even good-quality hay) contains some dust which reduces the amount of oxygen the lungs can absorb, which will reduce ➤

Feed enough forage to keep your horse happy and healthy.

performance. However, the longer you soak the hay, the more nutrients (calories and minerals and protein) you lose from it.

- Haylage is dust-free and an excellent source of fibre for the performance horse. It has a higher water content than hay, so more needs to be fed to meet the horse's fibre requirements.

- It is always a good idea to get your forage analysed at the beginning of the season

- If your horse is a good doer, then feed a low-calorie forage but do not reduce the total bulk (fibre) fed.

Energy

A misunderstanding of energy causes more confusion when it comes to feeding the competing horse than anything else. Just remember that calories and energy are exactly the same thing. When you see the term 'energy' in nutrition, it's measuring calories, not the character of the horse.

Thus if you have a good doer that needs more 'oomph', simply feeding him more calories will be counterproductive as his system will store them as fat and his performance will deteriorate.

If you have a good doer who needs more 'oomph' simply feeding him more calories will be counter-productive.

Fast-release versus slow-release energy

We can provide calories in different ways, either as fast-releasing energy or slow-releasing energy, but increasing overall calorie intake will not improve the *attitude* of your horse, unless he needs the extra calories from a nutritional perspective.

If you have a 'normal' horse then generally you can feed a straightforward competition mix.

If you have a 'fizzy' horse, then provide his calories with a slow-releasing energy competition mix, utilising oil and fibre.

If he is laid-back, then look for a fast-releasing energy mix (cereals, starch) but they need to be low-intake competition products as he doesn't need *excess* calories.

Fat-scoring

You need to provide your horse with enough calories (energy) to maintain a covering of fat (so long as he isn't a fat score of 4, see below) for his health and for his work. Ideally, your horse should be at a fat score of 3 for optimal health and performance.

How to fat-score

- Divide your horse into three parts: his neck (everything forward of his shoulder blades), his middle (ribcage and forward of his hips), his bottom (hips, pelvis and tail bone).

- Score each area separately (0–5 modified).

Neck

- There should be no fat above his nuchal ligament.

- You should be able to feel his shoulder blade and follow the outline with your hand.

- There should not be any fat just behind his shoulder blade.

Middle

- Run your hand along his ribcage; the individual ribs should be easily felt and you should see them when he breathes in.

- Place your hand at 90 degrees to his backbone (a hand's width from his withers). It should curve over the top of the bone.

Bottom

- Cup your hand around his hip bone.

- Feel the bones at the top of his pelvis.

- Feel the tail bone

- His bottom should be rounded and form an upside-down 'C' when you view from behind.

If you can do the above he is eating enough calories and he has a fat score of 3.If you can see his bones, he's not getting enough calories; if you cannot feel his bones then he's too fat and is getting excess calories in his diet. His performance will be compromised in both scenarios.

TOP TIPS Hard feed

- Choose a feed appropriate for the work level of your horse.

- If he is in light work, then use leisure feeds.

- If he is competing and being schooled for an hour every day including jumping, then pick a competition feed.

- It is always best to feed small meals, so divide his total daily amount into a minimum of two feeds (three or four are better).

- Add some chaff, as it increases the number of chews the horse makes, which increases his saliva production and slows the passage rate of the food through his gut.

- If you feed more than 2kg of hard feed per meal, then feed your chaff separately.

Feed several small meals during the day when competing.

Fat-scoring is just as important for a performance horse as it is for a leisure horse. Weight-tape and fat-score your horse fortnightly and keep a record. Know the difference between fat and muscle, as you cannot change one into the other – they are two completely different tissues.

Feeding and health

You need to ensure that your horse has enough protein to repair and build muscle and other tissues, and also micronutrients such as vitamins and minerals to stay healthy and improve recovery times.

Without the correct balance of vitamins, minerals and antioxidants, your horse cannot use the energy that you are feeding him, as micronutrients are used as co-factors in the energy cycles at cell level. They are also necessary for tissue, bone and muscle repair. It is vital, even when you are cutting back on calories to maintain the correct proportions of body fat and muscle, to ensure that your horse still has enough bulk (fibre) and that his micronutrients and protein levels are balanced – and this is when a nutritionist is helpful!

As well as protein to repair and build muscle, you must also feed micronutrients such as vitamins and minerals.

Vitamins, minerals and antioxidants

- If you feed less hard feed than the manufacturer recommends (check the back of the bag for feed guidelines), then you will not provide your horse with the recommended level of essential micronutrients.

- All hard feeds should be thought of as 'balancers' as they provide or balance the nutrition that would otherwise be missing in forage.

- Forage should always be the foundation for the diet; the better quality the forage, the less 'balancing' required.

- The calories can be supplied as fast release (like fruit sugar for us) which is broken down in the small intestine, or slow release (like pasta for us).

- A 'fizzy' horse needs more calories in ratio to his vitamins and minerals compared to a more laid-back type as he uses up more energy simply being 'him'. Both horses need the same amount of vitamins and minerals, but different quantities of calories to balance the forage. If your horse is in medium work, do not feed a leisure feed as it will not provide the correct amount of vitamins/minerals/electrolytes and antioxidants for work.

- Choose a low-calorie performance feed for a laid-back character or one that contains slow-releasing calories for a 'fizzy' type if you don't want to exaggerate your horse's natural character.

- Remember that horses need starch, vitamins and minerals to replace what is lost from the muscles after exercise, so a leisure feed will not be good enough for a horse in work.

- Excess calories/energy, regardless of how they are delivered, make a horse fat, and a deficiency causes him to lose weight; both reduce performance.

Hydration and electrolytes

Even mild dehydration results in suboptimal performance. For example, water loss equivalent to 1–2 per cent of bodyweight, (5–10kg in a 500kg horse), may reduce performance, while a 3–4 per cent water loss reduces performance by 5–20 per cent. The decrease in performance parallels the rapidity with which dehydration develops.

You might be surprised how much water your horse loses even when he is starting out in eventing. Remember that travelling can also result in dehydration, so bear this in mind, particularly in hot weather and on longer journeys.

TOPS TIPS Horse hydration

- Teach your horse to drink on the lorry and stop every hour to offer him a drink.

- Get into the habit of noting how much water your horse drinks at home.

- Flavour your water at home with squash and take it with you to competitions, to disguise the change in water flavour when you travel.

- If you are travelling a long distance, try to arrive at least the day before the competition to allow your horse to rehydrate.

- Check that your performance feed contains enough electrolytes.

- Remember to pack electrolytes to offer if your horse sweats up (continue to do so for 3–4 days to replenish the losses, but make sure the horse drinks water first).

- Use a scientifically validated weight-tape to monitor your horse's dehydration. 'Weigh' before and after travel and before and after cross country; this will tell you the amount of fluid your horse has lost.

Make sure you take enough water.

Feeding when travelling

As your move up the competition ladder, you will need to travel further to compete. Travelling uses up the same amount of energy/calories as the same hours of walking, so remember that your horse will be tired after a long journey.

TOP TIPS **Feeding when travelling**

- Try to keep feed times the same, even on competition or travel days.

- Generally, most people feed at the same times as usual, but provide smaller quantities if they are travelling.

- Haynets on lorries (fed dampened) will help to keep the digestive system healthy and the horse occupied.

Haynets will help to keep your horse occupied on the day.

5

KEEPING YOUR HORSE IN GOOD SHAPE

Keeping your horse in tiptop shape is important if you want to compete. In this section you'll find information on equine physiotherapy, farriery, dental care and tack.

Physiotherapy

Equine physiotherapy can help to ensure that your horse is ready to compete when you are, by treating and helping to prevent injuries. It maximises movement and function using applied knowledge of physiology, anatomy and biomechanics.

Physiotherapy can help prevent injuries as well as treat obvious problems.

Event horses are athletes and, like human athletes, they'll tweak and sprain muscles during preparation and at competitions. It's important that these mild tweaks and sprains are treated early so they don't develop into more major problems, which then require more treatment and time off.

Chartered Physiotherapists work closely with owners, riders and vets to look at the whole picture to help resolve any problems.

TOP TIPS **Check that your physiotherapist:**

- Is a fully qualified, chartered animal physiotherapist (anyone can set up as an animal physiotherapist without qualifications).

- Only works with veterinary referral (legislation means that before a physiotherapist treats your horse, they should get your vet's permission).

- Has professional and public liability insurance.

- Will liaise with other professionals such as vets, saddlers, farriers, and behaviourists if necessary.

- Adheres to the Chartered Society of Physiotherapy's Regulations and Standards of Practice.

To find your nearest qualified chartered animal physiotherapist, look online at www.acpat.org.uk

When could physiotherapy help?

- Soft tissue injuries to tendon, ligament and muscle.
- Back pain related/unrelated to lameness.
- Poor/inconsistent performance issues.
- 'He's not quite right'.
- Wounds and scar tissue.
- Splints, swellings and capped hocks.
- Behavioural issues.
- Lameness.

- Rehabilitation post-surgery.

- Age-related stiffness.

- Schooling/jumping problems.

- Sporting injuries.

- Prevention of injuries.

- Post-competition to promote tissue recovery.

Back problems

Muscular back problems are among the most common problems and can present in many ways. Often it's a change from the normal, for example, your horse is usually stiff to the right and has started being stiff to the left.

Like humans, horses will tolerate levels of pain very differently so it's important to get them checked and assessed and treated regularly to keep them pain-free and performing to their best.

Muscular back problems are one of the most common injuries.

Signs and symptoms of back problems

- Loss of performance.

- Schooling issues, disunited in canter, hollowing in transitions, lack of bend, inconsistency in the contact, reluctance to engage and use hind limbs.

- Change in temperament.

- Behavioural issues, bucking, rearing, nappiness.

- Jumping issues, refusing, unable to take off when deep, rushing.

- Resenting being saddled, 'cold-backed'.

- Lameness.

- Lack of straightness, especially going down hills.

- Dislike of being groomed.

Causes and treatment of muscular back problems

The most common cause is trauma, like falls, slips or getting cast. Horses can do stupid things, especially playing in the field! Badly fitting saddles are a common cause, so it's important to have the saddle and its fit checked regularly by a master saddler. In early spring event horses change shape as the work intensity increases, so it's is a good time to get saddles checked.

Referred pain

Muscular back pain can be a secondary problem caused by a primary problem in the limbs, such as a foot imbalance or joint problems like arthritis or navicular. Horses will compensate for the limb problem by holding themselves differently through their neck and back, causing them to go into spasm. The limb problem may be very mild, so no lameness is apparent. Although, with treatment, the back pain may resolve, it's likely to recur unless the cause of the problem is identified and addressed.

What treatment to expect

One of the most important tools a physiotherapist has is their hands. There are a wide variety of manual techniques used, such as reciprocal inhibition, trigger point release, myofascial release, joint mobilisations, massage and stretches. These will reduce pain, muscle spasm and stiffness, which in turn will improve range of movement and flexibility.

They also use electrotherapies such as ultrasound, LASER (light amplification by stimulated emission of radiation), PEME (pulsed electro magnetic energy) H Wave, TENS (transcutaneous electrical nerve stimulation) and neuromuscular stimulation. These are used to promote the body's natural healing processes, reduce pain and complement the manual therapies used.

Rehabilitation

Chartered physiotherapists are also involved in the rehabilitation of horses following injury, which is important to increase muscle strength and flexibility, with the aim to try and prevent recurrence of the injuries.

Your physiotherapist can show you a series of stretches for your horse to improve his flexibility.

You can help your horse by trying to improve his strength and flexibility using specific ridden and groundwork exercises. Your physiotherapist can give you a specific programme using lungeing or pole work, and teach you stretches for the neck, back and limbs to keep your horse supple and flexible.

TOP TIPS Prevention is better than cure

- Good warm-ups and cool-downs are essential.

- Work your horse in a way that's appropriate to his level of fitness and ability.

- Have regular physiotherapy, saddlery and dental checks.

- Don't ignore slight problems or small signs and symptoms.

Farriery

Shoeing intervals

The adage 'no foot, no horse' is never truer than when it comes to competing! Your shoeing schedule should come top of your list when planning your competition calendar. Book a schedule of appointments with your farrier every four to six weeks to ensure your horse's feet are in tip-top condition.

Horses' feet grow faster in the summer than in the winter, and some horses' hooves grow faster than others, so shoeing intervals will vary. Any longer than six weeks and you may encounter problems with lost shoes, degraded stud holes, long toes and imbalanced lameness, which all lead to avoidable annoyances, delays and cancellations that interfere with your competition schedule.

As you progress through the season and enter more events, you may find your farrier's appointments clash with your competitions. Think of bringing an appointment forward a few days or delaying it until after the event. This is especially important if you know your horse has a foot imbalance, weak heels, or is a full Thoroughbred with more sensitive feet. If you are on regular four to six week appointments a slight delay should not be a problem. The important thing is to have regular contact with your farrier who can

If you can't find the farrier on site, go to the secretary who will call him on the radio for you.

advise and work with you to help achieve your goals and keep you competing throughout the season.

If you're looking for a farrier, call the Farriers Registration Council who list all qualified farriers, or look them up online at www.farrier-reg.gov.uk

Studs

There's great debate about studs and their use. Some farriers and vets recommend the use of two in each shoe to ensure that the horse is evenly balanced, whereas others may recommend two in the front and one in the hind shoes, so that a horse can pivot more easily on landing after jumping a fence. Every horse is different – and indeed a farrier would stress that every *hoof* is different – so it's important to discuss your requirements with your farrier prior to the start of the season so that you can plan accordingly.

What all parties agree on, however, is that it's important to treat studs with caution. You need to practise jumping in studs in wet and dry conditions, so that you and your horse know what to expect, as a horse will change his way of going. If in doubt, always under-stud your horse and make that a rule of thumb. Many of the call-outs farriers have at events are because of the incorrect use of very large studs.

Always bear in mind that horses' forefeet need to slip a little as they land over a fence, to reduce the extreme stresses which are placed on the limbs at

the moment of impact. For this reason, you should never use very large studs in the front shoes.

For hard ground, you need studs that are pointed to penetrate it – like running spikes for runners. The harder the ground, the sharper and shorter the stud needs to be. For wet or more slippery conditions a bigger surface area is needed, so a bigger and fatter stud is more suitable. Some studs are a hybrid, designed for when there has been a recent shower or heavy dew on hard ground, giving a greasy surface on a hard base.

As a general rule, the smaller and lighter the horse, the smaller the studs you should use: the impact of a large stud on a smaller, lighter animal will be more extreme than on a heavier one. If in doubt, start with the smallest suitable studs for the conditions, as you can always try larger ones if you don't feel you have enough grip.

Various studs are available for different ground conditions.

How to use studs

- Don't keep your studs for more than a season as repeated use will damage the threads, making them difficult to screw in and out.

- Ensure you have a variety of studs – and spares – for all ground conditions.

- Use pointed studs on hard ground and blunt-ended ones on softer ground.

- Use smaller studs in the front shoes and larger ones in the hinds.

- Don't over-stud – they're not there to stop a horse in his tracks. Apply caution, and if in doubt *always* use smaller studs.

- Don't leave studs in your horse's shoes between phases; take them out immediately you get back to the lorry park. Remember a horse can kick out at any time with excitement or at a fly and injure himself, you or your helper.

If in doubt, always use smaller studs.

- Never leave a horse on a hard surface with studs as he'll feel very un-balanced.

- If you need to ride on a hard surface, like a road, to get to individual phases and you have your studs in, try to keep to the verge to avoid slipping.

- Use a smaller stud for dressage than you would for the jumping phases.

- Ideal packing for a stud hole is natural sheep's wool soaked in engine oil!

- Remember to re-plug the stud holes between each phase, otherwise you risk blocking them with stones and dirt.

- The best and cheapest tool to get the packing out of the stud hole and clean it out is a farrier's nail. Invest in a small wire brush to clean out the hole and threads.

- Keep your studs and tools together in one place – a plastic food container or small tin is ideal. You can also buy a magnetic metal dish to keep your studs and tap together safely in one place while you're at an event.

- Brush your studs off with your wire brush to clean them and then wrap them in an oiled cloth to keep them rust-free and ready for the next event.

- For your studs you'll need an implement with a stud tap to rethread your stud holes if necessary, and a spanner hole to tighten and loosen them, or an adjustable spanner.

Equine dentistry

When looking for a dentist, be sure to employ a qualified equine dental technician (EDT) or specialist vet. Check on the British Association of Equine Dental Technicians' (BAEDT), or World Wide Association of Equine Dentistry's websites for approved EDTs in your area.

Horses' teeth do not grow; they have a finite amount of tooth which migrates towards the chewing surface at the same rate at which it's worn away (2–3mm/yr).

If you're experiencing schooling issues such as head-tossing, tension, refusal to accept the bit, or you notice your horse dropping food out of his mouth (quidding), have his teeth examined. It's important to have him checked every 6–9 months, as sharp edges, hooks and mouth discomfort can all impair his general wellbeing and ultimately his performance.

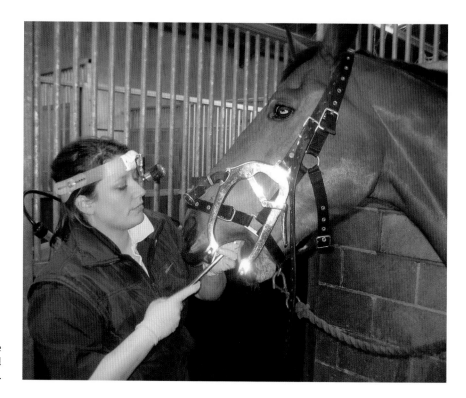

It's important to have your horse's teeth checked every 6 to 9 months.

Common tooth problems

Sharp edges

Sharp edges or cusps will naturally develop over time, and can cause soreness, lacerations and ulcers to the sides of the cheeks and to the tongue. Often horses with sores from these sharp cusps will find it painful to chew, so they give up and spit out a half-chewed ball of hay or feed. The cavesson part of the noseband presses the soft tissue of the cheeks over the sharp edges on the teeth, which can cause considerable trauma when riding.

Wolf teeth

Wolf teeth come in many different shapes and sizes. Usually they are short-crowned with a root two to three times the length of the crown and are found just in front of the first upper cheek tooth. They may interfere with the soft tissue and/or mouthpiece of the bit. They can be removed under sedation by your vet or a qualified EDT. Unerupted or displaced wolf teeth, or those found in the lower jaw, are usually problematical and nearly always need to be extracted.

Dental overgrowths

Dental overgrowths such as hooks, ramps, steps and waves usually develop because of a misalignment of the molars. They can restrict the forwards, backwards and side-to-side movement of the jaw, making establishing an outline painful, and can cause extreme discomfort and soft tissue trauma, often leading to quidding, weight loss, choke and even colic.

Gum disease

Gum disease affects around 60 per cent of horses over the age of fifteen. It occurs as a result of food becoming trapped between the teeth, which may be caused by age (as the roots of the teeth taper towards the base), misalignment or malpositioning of teeth, sharp edges and teeth that have not received adequate care. Gum disease is thought to be very painful for the horse, especially when bitted. It's possible to treat the early stages via referral to a specialist equine veterinary practice which offers advanced periodontal therapy.

TOP TIPS Dentistry

- Be sure that the person looking after your horse's teeth is qualified and a member of BAEDT, or a level two member of WWAED.

- Keep to the appointment schedule recommended by your EDT (check your insurance policy).

- Keep your horse's diet as natural as possible, with plenty of fibre fed from the floor; if your horse has dental problems, your EDT may advise specific feeds.

- Be sure your horse's tack fits and is necessary; over-tight nosebands can cause trauma.

- A horse that is not eating is a potential veterinary emergency; if your horse is displaying signs of a tooth problem, don't delay in seeking professional advice.

- Dental treatment needs to be regular and thorough in order to prevent future problems.

Your EDT visit

- Don't be startled by the amount of equipment used by the EDT; they are well trained and use it daily.

- Most EDTs routinely use electric or battery-powered dental instruments with diamond tips; these are highly efficient and very safe in the right hands.

- Most horses readily accept dental treatment, but some may require light sedation in order to get the very best possible job done. Sedation must be administered by your vet, or they may prescribe a gel for you to use beforehand.

Tack

Bits and bridles

The comfort and welfare of your horse is of prime importance – especially when competing, as that's when you put more pressure on your horse to perform at his best. So take your time when considering the array of bits and bridles available and remember to look at the Equipment Rules for Eventing to see what's acceptable for each phase.

Nosebands and martingales can completely change the action of a bit, so care is needed when fitting your bridle for both comfort and effect.

A bridle and bit work by acting together on the following sensitive areas:

1. The poll

2. The nose

3. The chin groove

4. Lips and corners of the mouth

5. The bars of the mouth (a sensitive part of the membrane of the mouth)

6. The tongue

7. The roof of the mouth

Remember to take all the bits you need for each phase if you are using just the one bridle.

Fitting a bit

Irrespective of the overall size of your horse, his shape, general condition and mouth size need to be assessed. Bits are made in a number of sizes, from 9.0cm (3½in) to 15.0cm (6in), in 0.5cm (3/16in) stages.

A snaffle bit should fit so that about a thumb's width shows on either side of the mouth when the bit is held with the joint (if it has one) flat.

The thickness of the mouthpiece is important and your choice may also depend of the breed of your horse, as a Thoroughbred may have leaner lips, tongue and bars whereas a Warmblood may have a thicker tongue, therefore not giving as much room for the mouthpiece. But it is also important to consider that thin mouthpieces are more severe in their action than thick ones.

The majority of bits are made of non-rust alloys, rubber, plastic or nylon. Check that there are no blemishes or rough edges on the bit, especially at the angle of the mouth. That's why an eggbutt joint is often preferred to the loose-ring to stop the lips being cut or pinched. Remember to check the BE rules for a description of what bits are permitted for each phase.

Consider the breed of your horse when fitting a bit.

TOP TIPS **Bitting**

1. Know your horse's mouth conformation before selecting his bit.

2. Understand the basic mechanics of the bit, its action and effect.

3. Bit according to your and your horse's ability.

5. Know the impact of nosebands and martingales upon the bit and don't over-tighten nosebands.

6. Make sure that the bit you select is the right width for your horse, as an ill-fitting bit will cause pain and damage your horse's mouth.

8. Introduce a new bit to your horse from the ground first, before you ride with it.

9. Have your horse's mouth and teeth routinely checked by an equine dental technician (EDT) or vet.

10. Make it part of your routine to wash the bit after every use and inspect your tack for any damage.

Check which bits are permissible for each phase in the BE *Members' Handbook*.

Saddlery

You'll be fine competing in a general-purpose saddle for all phases of your chosen event, so long as it fits you and your horse well. Remember, however, that as your horse gets fitter and develops more muscle tone across his back, the fit of your saddle will change.

If you are aiming to do a spring event and have not done much with your horse through the winter apart from light hacking, his body shape will have changed dramatically! So get your saddle checked by a Society of Master Saddlers Registered Saddle Fitter a few weeks before your event to make sure it is a still a comfortable fit, and not tipping forwards, backwards or slipping sideways.

As you progress through the eventing season, get your saddle checked again as your horse may put weight on during the summer, as well as increasing his general fitness, which can lead to another change of shape.

TOP TIPS Saddle fitting

- Any alterations, like flocking, rebalancing or strap replacement must be done by a qualified saddler.

- Your saddle must fit level. Looking from the side, the centre of the seat must be the lowest part.

- When you are sitting on the saddle there should be clearance of the pommel before and after you've ridden.

- The gullet of the saddle should be sufficiently wide to allow clearance along the horse's spine.

- Bear in mind that, if you use thick pads under the saddle for cross-country, it will have an effect on the fit of your saddle.

6

RIDER FITNESS AND MENTAL PREPARATION

You owe it to your horse to be as fit as you can when you want to compete. You can try walking, running or swimming to increase your fitness levels and Pilates to aid your balance and position in the saddle. Attention to correct nutrition is important in maximising your fitness and wellbeing, and a positive psychological approach will help you perform to the best of your ability.

As a general guide, you shouldn't be puffing more than your horse after jumping a course of showjumps in your field or arena. If you are, you need to think about your own fitness, as not only will it impair you on the day, but you could be setting yourself up for disaster if you are very unfit. General chores such as mucking out, leading your horse to his field twice a day and filling nets all help, but you need to think of fitness work beyond that to ensure you are not too tired to complete all three phases. A tired rider will struggle with balance, which can adversely affect the horse.

The good news is, you don't need to take out a gym membership or even buy an exercise DVD, but what you do need to do is incorporate some fitness work into your daily routine. In all, at a one-day event with one horse you'll probably be riding for about seventy-five minutes; that's based on a thirty-minute dressage warm-up followed by a four-minute test, a fifteen-minute showjumping warm-up followed by a two-minute round then a ten-minute cross country warm-up followed by an average five-minute round,

You need to be fit so as not to hamper your horse.

give or take a few minutes, with a little time added for riding back and forth from the horsebox park to the various arenas. Total time is likely to be longer if you have to add walking and settling exercises with a young or excitable horse. Bearing this in mind, you owe it to your horse – and yourself – to get a little fitter. Try out a few of the following exercises, starting your programme about six to eight weeks before your event to really reap the benefits.

Cardiovascular exercises

Fitness work

Stairmaster

Getting your heart rate up in short bursts is important as that helps to improve your fitness levels over time. One of the easiest – and most effective ways – is to use your stairs at home, office or school as a piece of fitness equipment. As well as being a great cardiovascular exercise, it helps to

tone your glutes (bottom) and legs, which helps when riding with shortened stirrup leathers when you are in your two-point seat for jumping and on the cross country course.

Six weeks before your first event, start off by running up and down the stairs twenty times in total every day, ten times in the morning and ten times in the evening. Increase this by a few flights every week until you are cruising up and down the stairs with ease. Once you feel fitter, you can increase the stair challenge by wearing your full cross country kit, including body protector and boots.

Pathfinder

Instead of slouching around the yard to pick up brushes or skips, or walking to the field to get your horse, try brisk walking or running. To get fitter, you need to increase your heart rate. You can also try jogging around the lanes or roadways or up and down local footpaths or bridleways in your area. Make sure you wear a pair of trainers rather than your boots. You'll soon feel better in yourself after just a week of running, even if it is only for ten minutes a day.

Keeping yourself fit is vital
if you want to compete.

Any cardiovascular exercise is good, so if you have an old bike in the garage, dust if off and get cycling! Work out a few routes – perhaps your usual weekend hack distance – and cycle it first before getting on your horse to ride it!

Swimmer

There is no better way to improve your fitness level in a gentle way while exercising your whole body than swimming! Head to your nearest pool twice a week, working up to three times a week, and feel your fitness levels soar! Aim for twenty lengths or half an hour in the pool to start with, using whichever stroke you feel most comfortable with. Ideally, use one or two different strokes, like breaststroke and backstroke to work the different parts of your body.

TOP TIP **Progression – intensity v. volume**

As your fitness levels increase, you need to decide how to continue to improve, by increasing either the intensity (how hard it is) or the volume (number of lengths swam, distance jogged or the time taken).

If you have a limited amount of time to exercise, or you are a ➤

person who likes an increasing challenge, then you will need to increase the intensity of the exercise to improve your fitness.

An easy way to do this is to add bursts of energy, so if you are jogging, add in intermittent thirty-second sprints then return to your jogging speed. The frequency will depend on you. Start with just one or two then build up. Do the same in swimming and cycling. If you are at a gym you can increase the level of difficulty on the fitness equipment, such as a slope on the running machine, up a level on the rower or cross trainer.

If time is not an issue, or you prefer building your endurance rather than getting all hot and sweaty, then you will need to increase the volume of what you do while keeping the intensity, or difficulty level, the same.

Pilates

Pilates exercises are great for strengthening key muscles in the body to aid your balance and position. Pilates works by strengthening the stabilising muscles of the body which improves your core strength. As well as working on your body, Pilates also heightens the mind-body connection, which in turn can create more feel. You'll start to move and flow in the saddle more naturally, at one with the horse – absorbing and responding to your horse's movement.

Try the following top five Pilates exercises for eventing – there are no excuses not to – you can use a towel on the floor if you haven't got an exercise mat.

Bucket tilts

You need to be flexible and allowing through your pelvis so you can move with your horse. If you are stiff in your lower back and pelvis, you'll block the movement from your horse, which can lead to him hollowing his back. Sitting on the edge of a chair, imagine your pelvis is a bucket, and you want to slowly and carefully tip a little bit of water out of the front, then the back, then each side – evenly! Try just a few tilts at first, working up to 8–10 each way. Don't force the tilts, but allow your lower back to move, bone by bone and really feel your lower spine gently freeing up.

Oyster

This is a great exercise to mobilise your hips and strengthen the muscles around them, whilst challenging the stability of your upper body. Strong gluteus medius (side of hip/bottom) muscles are essential for pelvic stability. Weakness can often be the cause of hip-hitching or crookedness in the saddle.

From side-lying, position yourself with your arm lengthened out underneath you, a cushion placed on top and your head rested down on the pillow. Your other hand can be either on your hip, ensuring your hips remain stacked one on top of the other with the waist long, or placed down in front of you. Have your back, bottom and feet in line with your mat and your knees bent and together, in your riding-leg length. As you open and close your leg, imagine pressing your thigh forwards and up, with your feet one on top of another. You should feel the muscles on the side of your hip working after 8–10 repetitions.

Oyster. Make sure that your hips are directly one above the other and that you are not leaning back or forward; you must be in alignment!

Squats

This exercise is great for strengthening your forward seat position for cross country. It increases the strength and balance in your legs and helps to mobilise the hips, knees and ankles. It's easy to fix and brace in this position if you're not used to it, which can lead to cramp and stiff knees and ankles. Ideally squat down to your riding leg-length for better effect – it's often lower than you think!

From standing, arms at your sides, lengthen out from your spine, reaching up with the crown of your head, pushing away the floor with your feet, then brush your thighs with your open palms as your arms swing forwards and upwards to almost shoulder height, as you bend your knees. Press down into your heels, keeping your upper body lengthened away. Hold for five seconds, then go back to the start, swinging your arms back into position by your sides.

Try to squat into your cross country position, and hold for 5 to 10 seconds.

Swimming

You need to lie on your front for this and the action you need is to lift your opposite leg and arm, making a swimming action – your arms and legs need to move in opposites, a little as though you are doing the front crawl.

First, make sure you are using your tummy muscles before you lift off an opposite arm and leg. Legs should be lifted from the thigh, not the knee, and arms from the shoulder. Hover each arm and leg about 10cm off the ground about 10–12 times each. You should feel this in your bottom, thighs and shoulder. If you feel it in your lower back, you must stop and engage your tummy muscles again, and check that you're not lifting your arms and legs too high.

Thread the needle

Flexibility is key in the saddle. Often as you get older or become more fixed in your position, rotation of the upper body becomes more difficult and flexibility can be lost. A strong centre is essential when your body goes suddenly off balance, like following an awkward jump or buck, and you need to recover quickly.

Kneel on the floor on all fours and place your hands so that your shoulder is directly above your wrist, hip above knee. Lengthen your spine out from the top of your head through to your seat bones, then transfer the weight of your upper body into one arm as you lift your other hand and arm and thread it through underneath you, rotating your upper body down and sideways, bending the standing elbow as you thread your arm through, watching your hand, so you turn your neck also. Repeat on each side 8–10 times.

Thread your arm underneath you, feeling the stretch along your ribcage.

To finish the movement, reach your arm away above you, increasing the stretch along the ribcage. A great exercise for increasing flexibility.

TOP TIPS Position in the saddle

- Legs moving back and forth? – You need to develop more pelvic stability. Try Oyster and Squats.

- Arms and hands won't keep still? – Develop your upper body stability and you will improve. Try Pilates Swimming and Thread the Needle.

- Leaning back or tipping forwards? – Check that your pelvis isn't tilted too far one way or the other; try the Bucket tilt exercise.

- Bumping on your horse's back? – You need to absorb more of the horse's movement through your lower back, by becoming more flexible, like a shock-absorber. Try Thread the Needle.

Pilates helps improve your balance and thus your position in the saddle.

Nutrition

Nutrition isn't just relevant to your horse! It's important that you think of yourself as an athlete too and therefore take care of what you eat and drink.

A really careless approach to nutrition may not simply lead to a below-standard performance, in extreme cases, such as very low blood sugar or dehydration, it may actually represent a safety issue.

DIETARY TIPS Nutrition notes

- **Drink plenty of fluids.** Even mild dehydration can make you feel tired and your body function less efficiently.

- **Eat breakfast.** Your liver glycogen stores reduce overnight and the brain relies on these for fuel. Some carbohydrate in the morning, like cereal, toast or a banana, will help raise your energy levels and thus reduce tiredness.

- **Eat regularly and don't skip meals.** This will help maintain your energy levels more evenly throughout the day. Eat smaller amounts more frequently rather than just one large meal per day.

- **Eat a healthy diet.** Make sure you eat plenty of fruit, vegetables, wholegrain foods, lean meat, fish and low-fat dairy products.

- **Eat iron-rich foods.** Iron is a constituent of haemoglobin, which carries oxygen from the lungs to the working muscles. Essential foods to include are red meat, dark poultry, liver, egg yolk, green leafy vegetables, nuts, seeds, beans (including baked beans) and lentils.

- **Take care with caffeine.** This includes coffee, tea, cola and stimulant drinks. A caffeine drink in the morning can boost energy levels and alertness, but more than five or six cups per day may lead to anxiety, irritability and reduced performance. If you have trouble sleeping avoid caffeine in the evening.

- **Your competition diet.** A new regime should never be tried for the first time at your first event – try it out a couple of times when, for example, you change your routine, like when you go cross country schooling. When you start to feel the benefits, looking after your own nutrition will soon become second nature.

Many people water their horse but forget about themselves – even if you don't eat much on the day, remember to drink.

DIETARY TIPS **Menu suggestions**

Breakfast

- Low-fibre breakfast cereal or porridge, with low-fat milk and very ripe fresh fruit or tinned fruit in natural juices.

- Large fruit smoothie, made with puréed fruit, yogurt and milk.

- Granary or multi-grain toast with jam, honey and large low-fat yogurt or low-fat milkshake.

Lunches

- Pasta or noodles (white) with a little lean meat and/or vegetables.

- Chicken in a low-fat cheese, mushroom or tomato-based sauce and basmati rice or cous cous with vegetables.

- Spaghetti bolognaise.

- Fish pie.

- Smoothie with low-fat milk, low-fat yogurt and banana, mangoes, berries.

- Multi-grain bread filled with chicken, ham, tuna, salmon, egg or low-fat cheese.

Top-up snacks

- Sandwich with low-fat cream cheese, chicken, turkey, ham, tuna, jam or peanut butter.

- English muffins, pancakes or toasted crumpets with honey, syrup or sugar and cinnamon.

- Fruit and low-fat yogurt.

- Low-fat biscuits like Jaffa Cakes, fig rolls, Garibaldi.

- Rice cakes or low-fat crackers with banana or jam.

Sports psychology

What makes the difference between a novice and an expert? Obviously knowledge, experience and skill, but attitude is fundamental to being able to produce better performances. Self-belief and confidence in your strengths as a rider are key to developing expertise. Read on to find out how sports psychology can help.

Chunking

Chunking is where several actions that a novice might treat as three or four individual actions, are treated as one by an expert. This makes the action, quicker, smoother and – of key importance – more likely to be automated.

An automated action can take as little as 150 milliseconds to initiate and execute. Because your conscious thought processes are freed up by an automated response, they are free to work on more strategic issues like routes, time and fences.

Take the half-halt for example; when we first learn it, the action can be a bit laboured, slow and often ineffective. When learning a half-halt there are usually several actions, like sit, check and release, then leg, that are treated as combined, but separate actions. Because the actions are conscious they go via the brain, which means that the half-halt can take up to two seconds to be executed, instead of the 150 milliseconds of an automated skill.

So, when you are on a horse travelling at perhaps 400m a minute this can make a massive difference to the effect of the half-halt, like taking around 13m to execute as opposed to a couple of metres or so. If you think of this on an approach to a cross country fence you can see why strides go awry when you are *thinking* about your half-halt rather than just *doing* it. Other examples of automatic skills are riding transitions, adjusting stride length and responding to disobediences.

Riding is arguably 80 per cent about feel, so a full brain that's busy deconstructing what should be automated tasks will block out or slow down your reactions, as thinking disrupts feel and delays reactions. As a rider, you need to be in the here and now.

When under pressure, even the most experienced riders can sometimes revert to a novice approach, particularly those who have brought horses through the grades themselves and have worked through problems. It's not uncommon for a professional to suddenly start doubting or mistrusting

OPPOSITE If on first look a fence appears huge, squat down in front of it for a few seconds, then stand up again, miraculously it often appears smaller!

skills that they normally take for granted, or revert to thinking of their horse as they were as novices, forgetting genuineness or ability, and trying to take over.

TOP TIPS **Ride in the here and now**

1. When you practise, make sure you understand what the whole action feels like from the seat of your jodhpurs upwards and downwards; not in terms of individual body parts.

2. Group tasks into a 'chunk' of actions that has one key, meaningful word that describes the output you require. Choose positive words like 'flow', 'up', 'forward' to achieve what you want.

3. Rehearse the word in conjunction with the set of feelings that you need; you can do this anywhere and don't need to be on a horse (thus increasing your repetition rate and therefore your level and speed of generating automaticity).

4. Trust yourself and, if you should find that you are going back to basics, think *stop* and then the key action word that triggers the feel you need.

5. Trust your horse where appropriate – positive riding is always better than defensive riding.

6. If all else fails, just think *do* it and look up and outwards.

Performance enhancers – triggers

The night before a competition you realise you've forgotten how to ride! You can't even picture yourself getting on, let alone steering your way around a cross country course. Your mind is mush and you wonder how on earth you're going to cope. Sound familiar?

One way to help is to use triggers. A totally legal performance-enhancer! Use words that correspond to a positive event and are personal to you and your relationship with your horse.

Triggers are part of a suite of mental skills tools and form part of your preparation. Being well prepared means you feel in control; being in control reduces anxiety and improves performance. Triggers will initiate a set of actions that will automatically kick in when you think or do something.

Try to steer away from wristbands or talismans as they can get forgotten or fall off, leaving you helpless. So forget lucky socks! If you did well, *you* did it, not a sock, so remember *what* you did, *how* you did it and then translate that into relevant triggers to help you re-create the same performance.

When you have your good feeling or memory, rehearse it repeatedly wherever you are – on the couch watching TV, in the car, in the supermarket. Keep the phrase or action simple and tie it to a situation or emotional response that you want to manage.

To help reduce anxiety on the day, learn your dressage test well before the competition.

Dealing with physical ten:

Tension means you lose feel, causing
can be an instant way of releasing te
training, capture how your whole boc
body, remember which muscles are ii
the contact on the rein and the press
legs. Name that feeling and use it as a tr

Mental approaches

When the voice in your head is negative or
it with a word that allows you to remember
like times when you have won, or complered
simple phrase such as 'done it, seen it', can be very useful, and when used in
conjunction with the powerful tool of visualisation, it's even more effective.

When you suffer from a loss of concentration, use the Eight Steps to
Competition Confidence in the box opposite to bring your mind back to
the job and to the here and now, like 'Feel it, do it.' Triggers such as looking at

the detail of your immediate environment can be helpful for concentration, like the hair pattern on your horse's neck, the shape of his ears, or the smell of newly oiled leather.

TOP TIPS **Eight steps to competition confidence – FUN PARTY**

- **Feel it** – physical feeling or a mental state of confidence.

- **Understand it** – what made it happen, how/why did it happen?

- **Name it** – remember the moment, feeling or emotion and name it.

- **Practise it** – muscular feeling or mental state.

- **Action it** – wherever, whenever.

- **Rehearse it** – again and again so it is automated.

- **Trust it** – believe in it.

- **Yell it** – in your head, so it removes other thoughts!

Remember the good parts of a previous competition – don't dwell on the negatives as it can erode your confidence.

7

TRAINING FOR DRESSAGE

Here we look at the elements of the dressage phase and offer expert tips and training advice to help you get the best result.

Practising the elements

As you'll know from riding dressage tests generally, they are made up of sectors, which each have a mark out of ten (except that, for the walk on a free rein, the marks are doubled), and there are also collective marks, which are applied to the test as a whole. At the end of the test, the marks are combined then, in eventing, the total marks are deducted from the maximum possible to get the penalty score.

Preparation at home is really important if you are to get the best marks per movement that you can. Practise your centre line entrance, riding through the corners, 20m circles, diagonal lines and halts. Unless these movements become routine at home, you won't able to pull them off convincingly at an event.

When working on the flat, practise achieving a good rhythm in whatever gait you're riding, with a flowing, forward contact. Your transitions and turns should be balanced, supple and relaxed.

Concentrate on the Scales of Training (see What the Dressage Judge is Looking For) and create a dialogue between yourself and your horse by using your hands, legs and seat. You want your horse to be responsive and relaxed, and the best way to achieve this is to enjoy your training and reward him when he gets the hang of a movement and performs it well.

A good, enjoyable and relaxed experience in the first phase will set you both up for the jumping to follow.

The basics

Learning the test

You need to learn the test, as you can't have a caller. You're not permitted to carry a whip in the test itself and your horse mustn't wear boots in the arena. Remember to wear gloves, because these are compulsory items of dress.

Tests in current use are printed in the BE *Members' Handbook,* and you'll find the number of the test you need to ride at a competition detailed in the Event Schedule. BE80(T) competitors currently ride the same tests as those competing in BE90 classes.

Riders running through the pattern of the test before going in. Make sure you have learnt it as you can't have a caller.

Position

Ideally, your elbows should be in line with the heels of your boots. Hold your hands steady, with a giving rein. Lift your stomach and sit tall. Imagine someone is pulling your hair up towards the sky, lifting you up and out of your lengthened lower back – don't be stiff or bracing yourself. Feel your seat bones evenly on the saddle. Your legs should be resting against the horse's sides, heels in line with your hips and the balls of your feet resting in the stirrups, feet slightly flexed and weight through your heels, but not forced down.

TOP TIPS Rising trot

If you tilt forwards in rising trot, then use your bottom muscles to rise! This helps to stop the tilt forwards as you straighten your hip flexor muscles.

TOP TIPS Stability and stillness

Finding it hard to keep the arms independent of the body? Improve your upper body stability by lifting from the breastbone, and imagine that you have shrugged your shoulders down, rather than up, but don't brace or force them. Having your shoulder sitting back correctly without bracing your elbow allows your arm to work softly through the shoulder and elbow.

Centre line

In the test, coming up the centre line creates the judge's first impression of you and your horse – and also their final impression as you ride up the centre line to salute at the end of the test, so it's particularly important to practise doing it well. You can also use the same principles to ride diagonal lines when changing rein.

How?

When practising, use the three-quarter line as well as centre line, so both you and your horse get used to riding without the 'support' of the arena fencing or dressage markers on the outside track. Think of your centre line starting and ending with a corner, so it's your job to ride firmly and efficiently through this and accurately onto your line then to track smoothly left or right at the other end. Allow your legs to create a channel for the horse to go forwards and draw towards the judge's car at C. Keep yourself centred in the saddle and your core muscles strong as you fix on C and are pulled to it, as if being drawn up a tube.

When riding the centre line, don't think of speeding up to keep the straightness, but keep using half-halts to steady, balance and then ride forward. Your horse should follow your hands, so allow with your reins and squeeze him up to the reins and bit. Ride a half-halt on the exit of the preceding corner to set him up for the centre line and to help him stay balanced for the whole movement. Aim to start the turn a metre before the marker, thus allowing for his body length to turn through the corner.

Riding a turn

As you know, each dressage arena has four corners, and all changes of direction also involve riding a turn, so this is a really important movement to perfect at home.

Practise riding your turns in the arena or your field at home.

How?

Balance with a half-halt before you turn a corner or change direction. If you're not yet confident with half-halts, just steady the horse a little, so you can then ride forward through the turn. You should ride a corner like you would a quarter-circle, keeping your horse balanced throughout. Once you've started to turn, lighten the inside rein and allow the horse to finish the turn and ride forward to the new line. Your horse should bend evenly through his body when making a turn or corner.

If, when practising at home, your horse rushes or falls in through the bend, a good exercise is to make a transition to walk before the corner and encourage him to bend and listen through the corner. Then trot on again after the corner. Moving on, you can ride a half-halt before the corner and then ride forward through the turn.

Free walk on a long rein

Make this movement part of your everyday routine as it's a great way to encourage your horse to listen to your legs and not rely on your rein contact. It's important to allow your horse to stretch his neck down and release his muscles after a session in the school.

How?

Release the reins gradually as your horse stretches down. Fix your eyes on the point you are going towards and ride at it – this movement is not an excuse for a meandering walk – keep your horse straight with your legs firmly on his sides and drive him with your hips and your seat (although be careful not to *overuse* your seat, or your horse could fall onto his forehand and hollow, or he could rush). Don't restrict the walk, just allow it to happen.

A common mistake is to 'throw the reins' at the horse, who, if not used to the movement, will be surprised and in many cases will instantly lift his head, rather than stretch down. Another mistake noted by judges is that

---

TOP TIPS Extra marks

Double marks are up for grabs for your free walk on a long rein, so take time to improve it at home by incorporating it regularly into your flatwork sessions.

many riders don't give *enough* with the reins, which should really be on the buckle end. But have some light contact through the reins so your horse doesn't feel abandoned.

Trot and canter circles

Practise being as accurate as you can with your size of circle! A judge can see if you hit each point of the arena as you make your circle and will mark you accordingly. Accuracy marks are easy to pick up, so it pays to practise 20m circles at home – and not just in an arena as the majority of your dressage tests will be on grass, so get into your field and mark out a 20 x 40m arena.

A circle or turn must involve the horse from poll to tail and shouldn't just be a bend of the head.

How?

Before you start the canter movement, half-halt your horse to get him up together and listening. Use your legs to press him forward before you use your hands. Your inside hip should stay relaxed and move with him as you allow him to bend around your leg, giving with the reins.

As you move around the circle, your inside leg and rein create the bend; your outside rein is responsible for the correct bend and also prevents the horse from drifting. Always look around the circle to where you are going and your horse will follow.

Remember you're travelling at speed in canter and will cover the ground more quickly than in the other gaits, so plan ahead and allow for your horse's length as you approach each point of your circle, as it must hit the outside track on each side.

Halt

Make it your new rule always to ask for an accurate, square halt from your horse when training at home, even if you're just stopping to adjust your girth or stirrup leather. It then becomes routine for him and it's something horses learn very quickly.

Ask for an accurate, square halt.

How?

When you are working on transitions on a figure of eight in trot, walk over X, then halt, then back to walk and trot on again.

Another way is to work on half-halts down your centre line. If your half-halts are not yet established, ask your horse to halt and then, as he is about to stop, press him on again. This gets his attention and focuses him on what you are about to do, and also gets him thinking forward in the halt, rather than faltering to a stop and then stepping back.

As you progress with this exercise, start adding in some halts, by sitting deep, using your voice and giving with your reins. Your horse's reaction to the halt command should be to move forwards into it.

Give and retake the rein

This movement is occasionally asked for in eventing dressage tests. Essentially the judge wants to see a definite offering of the reins to the horse for three to five strides. It demonstrates that your horse is willing and working 'through' from your legs and is not relying on your hand, so when you give the rein he should carry on as if you still had the contact.

How?

Practise this across X in your arena. Get the feeling of giving the rein for a couple of strides only to start with, then quietly retake the reins. As you release the reins, bring the horse back with your seat by sitting back slightly.

What the dressage judge is looking for

The judge is looking for a horse working in a correct outline, in good balance, showing suppleness and obedience in all gaits. The horse should be trained according to the Scales of Training, which are:

Rhythm: Is the horse working in an even, clear rhythm throughout the test?

Suppleness: Does the horse show the same suppleness and flexion in each direction? A naturally stiff horse will have less suppleness than a naturally supple one, but this can be improved with training.

Contact: Is the horse working to an even and soft contact, showing a correct outline for the level of competition?

The judge is looking for a horse working in a correct outline, in good balance, showing suppleness and obedience in all gaits.

Impulsion: Is the horse working forward with energy from behind to propel him with contained energy throughout the test?

Straightness: Is the horse straight on either rein and bent evenly through his turns?

Collection: This would not be required until BE Intermediate level but it is something to aim towards. The horse should show only enough collection to carry out the required movements with ease.

Pointers for working with the scales of training

- Constantly check your progress with attention to the Scales, and improve areas that you feel are not as good as they could be. There's no point adding more energy (impulsion) if the rhythm, suppleness and contact are not established, as this will work against you. Create a dialogue with your horse between your hands and seat. You want your horse to be responsive but remain relaxed.

- When thinking about contact, ensure it comes from your elbows and not from your hands.

- In addressing straightness, think about keeping the horse's shoulders in front of his hips, not the hind legs behind the forelegs as this often makes you reverse the correct aids.

- Within these Scales try to ride as many full transitions (from one gait to another), or half-transitions (smaller steps to bigger steps and back again within the gait) as you can.

Dressage training tips

The following tips and exercises have been suggested by BE accredited coaches and top riders, so they are well tried and tested. Have a look on the BE website to find your nearest coach. You'll find the names of the contributing coaches listed in the Acknowledgements.

You don't need an arena for practising – a field is a good preparation for grass eventing arenas.

Suppling – spiralling using leg-yield

Try spiralling in and out, first based on a 20m circle, decreasing this to 15m when you and your horse both feel confident, first in trot and then canter. It's excellent for improving suppleness and also for helping you to ride different- sized circles accurately.

How?

Use your inside leg to create the bend and leg-yield your horse in and out on your circle, gently flexing your horse's head and neck to the inside and outside to improve his flexibility and prevent him from leaning on the reins.

When you are happy on the circles, try leg-yielding across the school from the outside track to the centre line then back again to the track on the long side – all valuable obedience preparation for your horse.

Encouraging your horse to listen with half-halts

One of the most important tools you have as a rider, which is useful for all phases, is the half-halt. It can add the 'wow' factor to your test as it helps to balance your horse, sit him back on his quarters and help prevent him running through the reins.

You can add a half-halt just before a corner, on the way out of a corner, before you turn onto the centre line or across the diagonal, or wherever it is desirable to improve your horse's balance and attention.

How?

To half-halt, sit a little stronger and more upright in the saddle and increase the contact on the reins as if about to ask for halt. The moment your horse responds, you need to let go immediately with your body and your reins, releasing the rein contact to where it was before you asked. Allow him time to react to the release. (A common mistake is to forget to give with the reins as soon as your horse 'sits up' and listens.) This takes a little practice, but you can perfect it at home in all gaits by adding it into your flatwork routine. Once you are in-tune with your horse, you'll feel him respond instantly to your command for a half-halt. It's very rewarding – plus you'll notice your dressage scores improve!

Transitions

Transitions are essential for every phase and you can never ride enough of them! A good routine to get into at home is to incorporate ten or so transitions in each gait, both up and down the gears, to get your horse thinking forward and listening to you.

Try walk-trot-walk, trot-walk-trot, walk-halt-walk, canter-trot-walk and so on. Remember to alternate what you ask for, so your horse does not start to anticipate a change of gait and then fall 'behind the leg'.

Change the place where you ask for transitions when schooling, so if you are in an arena, don't just ask for them on the outside track; ask on the three-quarter line and when on a circle or figure of eight. Many eventers are Thoroughbred or Thoroughbred crosses and tend to have longer than average backs. Transitions will help no end if you have a horse that can become quite strung-out in his movement.

Try to make your transitions from one gait to another as smoothly as possible.

How?

To ask for a transition, which alerts the horse to the fact that something is coming, sit deeper and stiller in the saddle and use your upward or downward aids clearly and confidently, so your horse understands just what you are asking for. Remember to reward your horse with a pat, or rub his neck when he performs well.

Accuracy with four circles

Judges consider the accuracy of each figure in a test as well as the quality of movement. When you are starting out, try to be as accurate as you can, and the quality of the movement will come the more you ride.

How?

Warm up with a free walk, allowing your horse to stretch down through both reins, and leg-yield from the centre line to the inner track in walk and trot.

– Starting in medium walk, on the right rein, walk a 10m circle at A, E, C and B.

– Change the rein with a free walk on a long rein.

– Repeat the walk exercise on the left rein, with a 10m circle at A, B, C and E.

– Change the rein with a free walk on a long rein.

– Working trot right rein; circle 15m A, E, C and B.

– Change the rein with a four-loop serpentine.

– Repeat the working trot circles on the left rein; 15m circle at A, B, C and E.

– Change the rein with a four-loop serpentine.

– Allow the horse to stretch down in walk, on both reins.

– Working canter right rein; circle 20m A, E, C and B.

– Change the rein with a simple change of leg over X ridden either on the diagonal line or down the centre line.

– Repeat the working canter circle exercise on the left rein; 20m circle A, B, C and E.

– Change the rein with a simple change of leg over X ridden either on the diagonal line or down the centre line.

– Afterwards, stretch your horse down on a long rein, in working trot on both reins.

TOP TIPS **Don't look down**

Say out loud what colour horse you have. He will always be that
colour, so you don't need to keep looking down at his shoulder
when you're schooling, as he won't change!

Sounds simple, but
remember to look where
you are going!

Rhythm

A regular rhythm is important for all phases and it is important that you become familiar with your horse's movement and are able to regulate it when you need to most – for example, a 'coffin canter' for combination fences, or a 'power canter' for a steeplechase fence. In dressage you need to demonstrate a regular rhythm in all gaits, with your horse using his body correctly, in balance and not 'running through the rein'. It takes time to develop this, particularly if you are riding a young horse.

How?

Once you have established a good trot rhythm, use the letters down each long side in the school, KEH and MBF, and count the number of trot strides you take between two of the letters, K and E, and then maintain the same number of trot strides between the other letters, E and H and then M and B, B and F. Regulate your rising trot by either slowing down the rise or quickening it to achieve regularity.

For the average horse you'll get five strides between each letter in a 20 x 40m arena.

Once you are happy with this, you can progress by adding or taking out a stride. Not only will this help to find your regular rhythm, but it's also an easy method of working towards medium or collected trot.

The exercise can also be done with equal effect in the canter, with generally three strides between the long-side letters in a 20 x 40m arena and it has the added benefit of teaching you to ride accurately to the letters, improving your eye and precision in the arena.

Don't limit the merits of this exercise to flatwork; it's a great exercise to use before a jumping session as it naturally helps you establish your gears.

OPOSITE For the salute, move your reins into your left hand, then bow your head and move your right arm down and back to your side.

TOP TIPS Points to remember

Perfect your half-halt. This will help set your horse up between movements, thus gaining you more marks. Don't expect your horse to do a movement at an event if you haven't practised and perfected it at home – it just sets you up for a disappointment. Whether practising in your field or arena, try riding the individual movements as accurately as you can.

8

TRAINING FOR SHOWJUMPING

Here we look at the elements of the showjumping phase and offer expert tips and training advice to help you get the best result.

Practising the elements

The number, height and types of fences for your chosen level are all regulated within the BE *Members' Handbook*. You'll meet 7–12 uprights, oxers, planks, spreads, ascending fences and one double combination (at BE100 level there will be at least one double combination). No water trays are used in BE80(T) to BE100; a square parallel is used on a BE100 course.

The maximum length of a BE showjumping course is 450m for BE90–BE100, and 400m for a BE80(T), with a speed of 325mpm.

You can practise all these fences at home or, if you don't have any poles, hire a local arena with fences. Have a play jumping a cross-pole from both sides to get your eye in and hone your accuracy skills. Next jump a few individual fences, bringing in spreads, oxers and uprights. Then string a few together to make a little course until you finally jump around all the fences, including a double, in a good rhythm.

Basic considerations

When you walk the course, walk exactly where you are going to ride, so you know where you'll need to adjust the power to jump particular fences, and also to keep within the time.

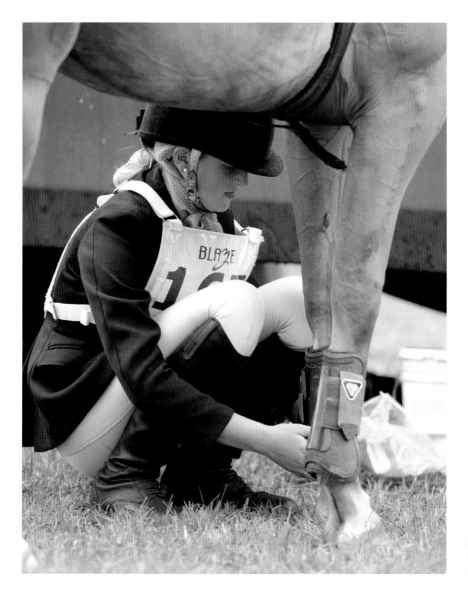

Remember to pack your choice of tendon boots for the showjumping phase.

To jump a course of fences, your horse needs to be supple and so the warm-up is important. Try riding him in canter with first an inside, then an outside bend. Incorporate leg-yield, so he responds to your leg commands the instant you put them on.

Establish your powerful, bouncy canter in the practice arena and take this into the ring. Don't allow the stride to get too long and flat as this will reduce your accuracy in your chosen line to the fence. To help do this, adjust your stride in canter on a circle; move your horse forward then bring him back, keeping him listening. Then try spiralling in and out of the circle with your leg.

Use your legs to push through the turns on the course, always looking ahead to your next fence.

Once he's listening, can hold his rhythm and is taking you forward, jump the cross-pole a couple of times before adding in the upright and a parallel.

Position and pace

Ideally, you don't want to be sitting too far over the horse's withers or too deep in the saddle, as you need to be comfortable in adjusting your balance in the saddle and over a fence. Your length of stirrup leathers for showjumping should not be as long as in the dressage phase or as short as for cross country.

When you jump, fold your body over the saddle, over your horse's neck, giving with the rein as you do so to allow him to stretch over the fence. Your coach can help you with your jumping position.

Use your legs to push though corners and lines on the course, and your hands and legs to regulate the canter (paying attention to both speed and stride length) and to keep the horse supple and bending. Try not to use your hands just as the stop button and the legs to go.

Components of a BE showjumping course

Upright fences

Sit tall when approaching an upright and squeeze – don't push. If you are jumping a double of uprights, keep your body upright going into the fence, then squeeze to get to the second part, holding your horse between hand and leg.

An upright tests your courage and precision as a rider, as you need to place your horse a little deeper than usual to the fence and sit and wait. If you push on you will only flatten your horse and he will knock off the top rail. If you find yourself going in too fast, just sit back – don't be tempted to 'throw' your horse at the fence.

Planks

Essentially a form of upright, these are a favourite of course designers. Although they can be positioned anywhere around the course, they are usually towards the end. By the time you reach the planks, very often your horse may have flattened a little and upped his speed, making it a more difficult fence to negotiate successfully. Planks can cause nervous or unprepared riders unnecessary penalties!

When walking the course, look at the ground on the approach to the fence – does it slope down and away, or up to the planks? How close are the other fences to it? Are you approaching on the left or right rein? Once you have considered these questions, you are instantly more prepared, as the most important thing to think about when approaching planks is balance and impulsion.

Oxer or parallel spreads

An oxer is a fence in which the front and back rails are of equal height, or the front rail is lower. A square parallel is a fence in which the height and spread are the same. A cross-pole spread with a rail behind is a little more forgiving than an upright or square parallel, but it tests your accuracy as you need to aim towards the middle of the fence. It's usually the first fence on the course to help get you set up.

Don't be temped to go flat out at the spread as, if you do, you will have the back rail off: approach an oxer in the same way as an upright.

It is important to ride forward when landing after an oxer or parallel and to drive your horse forward into your hand, keeping your rhythm.

Upright to a parallel

A favourite of course designers, this combination tests your ability to sit and wait for the first element and then squeeze or gather your horse up for the second element of the parallel and keep the poles up!

When approaching this line, keep your horse straight and your canter stride level all the way in and then, when you land, keep your horse 'in front of your leg' and think to yourself 'even-even-even' as you count the strides, almost getting your horse to bounce like a rubber ball between hand and leg.

Start as you mean to go on, in a positive frame of mind.

Double

As you approach the first part of the double, look up and sit up, balancing your horse. Squeeze with your legs in the last few strides to the fence to keep him moving forward. However, overcome any urge to 'throw him' at the fence, which can sometimes happen if you are anxious about making it to the second part of the combination.

Once you've taken off, focus on the second part of the double and sit up as soon as you land to set him up for the next part. Keep squeezing, but

Overcome the urge to 'throw' your horse at a double.

otherwise sit still and quiet in the centre of your saddle and wait for the second part to come.

Practise this at home by using 'V' poles on the fences, to help you aim for the middle and to encourage your horse to keep going forward. Place guide poles on the ground between the elements of the combination, which will encourage your horse to move on to the second part.

TOP TIPS **Don't worry about height or spread**

If presented well to a fence, you'll find that (within the bounds of reason) height makes no difference to your horse. The higher you jump, the more the horse will learn to balance himself better, meaning that, as a rider, you will have less to do.

Worried about spreads? Don't be! Consider the length of your horse, probably 2–3m from nose to hind foot. He can easily clear that width and more, so BE80(T), 90 and 100 will be no problem for him, as he covers more width than that in a canter stride.

TOP TIPS **Practise to be confident**

Practise jumping a hole or two higher at home than the height at the competition you have entered. If you have entered a BE90, then practise jumping, mastering and feeling comfortable over a few 1m courses at home – that way, when you get to your competition and walk your showjumping course, you will feel confident in both your and your horse's ability.

Confidence in the practice arena is essential and will help set you up for a good round.

Showjumping training tips

The following tips and exercises have been suggested by BE accredited coaches and top riders, so they are well tried and tested. Have a look on the BE website to find your nearest coach. You'll find the names of the contributing coaches listed in the Acknowledgements.

Depending on your horse's age and experience, use common sense to decide how many or which exercises to do until you are both more experienced. The difficulty level of an exercise often depends on the size of the area you are working in, as the smaller the area the tighter the turns and therefore the more difficult the exercise. So don't ask for more than what you or your horse is capable of at the moment, as all training should be gradual.

Obedience

Having your horse go where you want him to go and do what you want him to do is crucial in the showjumping ring. He must learn to wait, between hand and leg, while jumping around a course of fences.

How?

If possible, use your upper-body weight instead of your hands to shorten and lengthen your horse's stride and adjust his speed. You can practise this at home by getting your horse to lengthen and shorten in the school. Have a go at lengthening for five strides, then shortening for five strides, then four, then three.

Athleticism through gridwork

Jumping small fences or working over poles on the ground works wonders for both your balance and your horse's coordination. It will also improve your feel for a good canter rhythm.

While the fences are small, you can concentrate on your own position, allowing your horse to have a bit of fun whilst moving forwards through the grid. Remember, it is up to you to get the horse to the fence – it's his responsibility to jump it!

How?

Set up some poles on the floor spaced according to the size of your horse's stride and whether you want to approach them in trot or canter. (See Top Tips

– Trot and Canter Poles page 120 for more details.) Trot or canter through the grid, aiming for the centre of the fence to give your horse the best possible chance of making a clean jump. Keep steering him to the middle of the fence or pole all the way through.

Keep a regular trot or canter stride along the grid, not altering or changing the rhythm.

You can also vary the distance between each pole or fence, to change your horse's stride length. You can go from two strides to one or two to three or vary them along the length of the grid, thus increasing the challenge.

Once you've mastered going straight down the line and looked at different distances in between, try a few exercises like turning as you land over the last one.

Approach the grid on both the left and right rein and then track left or right when you have jumped the last fence in the line, which will help increase your horse's suppleness and reaction time, plus inject some variety. This will keep him listening to you as he doesn't know which way you want him to turn next. It's also a great exercise to encourage your horse to land on the correct leg.

Aim for the centre of the fences when practising at home, looking towards the next turn or fence.

TOP TIPS **Trot and canter poles**

Placing pole in front of a fence
Place this nine of your feet* end to end, or three of your strides away from the base of the fence.

Canter poles on the ground
Place them nine of your feet end to end, or three of your strides away from the base of the fence.

Trot poles
For two horse trot strides, place nine of your feet end to end, or three of your strides away from the base of the fence, same as canter.

For one horse trot stride in between, which is more the normal practice, place them 1.35m (four and a half of your feet, or 1½ human strides) apart.

For ponies, place the poles a little closer, 2.4–2.75m (about eight and a half of your feet) apart for two trot strides (although most bigger ponies can trot happily through a grid laid out for horses).

*Distance assumes that one of your booted feet's length is approx. 30cm (i.e. one foot) in length. Use common sense if your feet are much smaller or larger than this.

Suppling exercises

You won't be jumping grids at the event, but a number of individual fences and combinations on different reins, so it's important that you feel confident jumping a variety of fences, approaching from different directions and angles.

Figure of eight fences

How?
Set up a variety of small, single fences, varying your approach and line. Once you've mastered them, try riding a figure of eight, with a cross-pole placed

where the middle of the eight would be. Keep approaching the cross-pole on a different rein, thus improving your reaction times and strengthening your and your horse's ability to jump off either rein.

This exercise is great for excitable horses as it prevents them from running away from you and rushing their fences, because they have to turn so often. You can use your hands gently to balance your horse on those turns, but try to use your legs to keep him going forward.

Try to influence which leg your horse lands on as you jump by using your bodyweight. Come in a straight line over the fence, then ask him to bend and turn as he jumps over the poles. If you can influence him at this stage, then your showjumping rounds will become a lot smoother when you get to the ring.

You can build up this figure of eight exercise to incorporate more fences at the top and bottom of the eight.

Jumping exercise on a circle

How?

Once you have popped a few fences on both reins using the figure of eight exercise, move on to jumping your single fence on a circle. Just keep popping the fence, keeping your horse in the same, rhythmical canter all the way around. While doing these simple exercises, think of your own jumping position and try to balance yourself in the approach, when jumping and when moving away from the fence.

TOP TIPS Focus from start to finish

Never think of the last fence as the end of the course but merely as another fence, so that you ride each obstacle with equal focus.

Solving rushing

How?

When, approaching a fence in trot or canter, you feel your horse surging forwards, ride a downward transition to trot or walk to balance him, then close your legs, soften your arms and let your horse jump the fence. How-

Focus from start
to finish.

ever, if you feel totally out of control of his forward momentum, then turn him away from the fence and do a circle or two until you feel back in charge again. Then, ask him to approach the fence, this time on your terms. If he rushes, turn him away in good time (e.g. not right in front of the fence, but a good few strides away) and keep doing this until he gets the message that you are in control and not him.

Usually a horse that rushes his fences is doing so to compensate for something that happens in the process of jumping the fence, which could be you unbalancing him and affecting his jump. As a result he flattens and compensates with speed.

So, if you find your horse too strong, running away, or you feel you could do with a stronger bit, try a neckstrap first. Hold the neckstrap with your index finger, which will allow you to balance on that rather than his mouth, taking away his stimulus to run away.

Working with several fences

This exercise works on your horse's rhythm, and his agility to turn and jump fences at an angle whilst maintaining rhythm. Throughout the different steps of the exercise, you should maintain the horse's balance and rhythm, and make sure that the turns are made in a smooth, balanced, gentle manner.

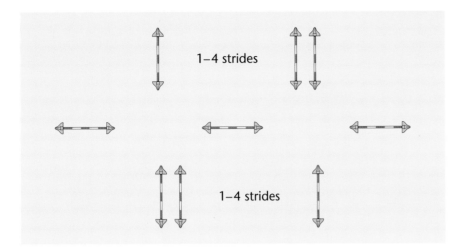

How?

Lay out some basic fences as in the diagram.

- On the flat, ride in walk, trot and canter, in and out of the fences on the centre line in a serpentine with varying degrees of depth to the loops. Whilst in canter, make transitions from canter to walk and back into canter when changing direction, or make flying changes, and use this part of the exercise to work on the horse's balance, obedience and suppleness.

- Jump the fences on the centre line at a 90 degree angle, riding a loop around the jumps on the long side.

- Jump the fences on the centre line at angles going inside the fences on the long side.

- Jump the fences on the long side in a straight line.

TOP TIPS Improve your steering

Just chop up your broken showjump poles to 1.2m each and put them on upright stands, blocks or buckets and get jumping over small fences – it doesn't matter how many you knock down as the aim of the exercise is to focus on steering and get a feeling for regular rhythm and speed – good luck and the only thing that really matters is that you enjoy it!

If you keep getting too deep to a showjump, consider a take-off point a metre away rather than the base of the fence.

> **TOP TIPS Correcting take-off**
>
> If you keep getting too deep to a showjump and knocking it down, look at the take-off point a metre away from the fence rather than the bottom of the fence. This changes your focus and really works.

9

TRAINING FOR CROSS COUNTRY

There's no substitute for getting out to a schooling ground and jumping a variety of cross country fences, but you can have a go at the basics of what you will meet on course at home.

Understanding the basics

Think of the cross country phase as a jigsaw puzzle. It's not just about the fences: as well as practising over a wide variety of obstacles, you need to think about the other pieces you need to master to complete the puzzle, and plan your training from there.

You must to be able to ride confidently in a rhythm in an open space, cantering your horse away from other horses. You need to have experienced riding up and down hills. You must have practised a bouncy, active canter for your combination fences and a powerful, forward-going canter for more open jumps, such as a steeplechase fence. You need to have addressed your own fitness and that of your horse and feel comfortable in your two-point seat or forward position off your horse's back. You also need to have an idea of your speed.

Know the course set-up

A cross country round at BE80(T)–BE100 will typically be 1,500–2,800m long, with 18–25 jumping efforts. The speed is set differently for each level and is measured in metres per minute. So the calculation for the optimum time is made by dividing the length of the course, using the line as a horse would jump it, taking all the direct routes, by the metres per minute set for that class. BE80(T) (purple flags) is set at 435mpm, BE90 (orange) is 450mpm and BE100 (pink) is 475mpm. Amongst other regulations, penalties are given for refusals, missed fences and falls. A full set of Rules can be found in the BE *Members' Handbook.*

Organisers direct horse 'traffic' along horse-walks.

TOP TIP **Measuring metres per minute**

Speeds required at basic level are:

BE80(T) – 435 metres per minute

BE90 – 450 metres per minute

BE100 – 475 metres per minute

To help yourself to get a feel for cross country speed, measure out a distance of 100 metres, using a marker at either end. This is usually best done at a cross country schooling ground where you will have plenty of room and a good grass surface on which to practise. You can use a measuring wheel, a tape measure or perhaps stride it out yourself having measured one of your average strides. Alternatively, you may have a field headland that runs alongside a road so you can measure 0.1km in your car. Once ready, approach the first marker in a good, forward-going canter, in your two-point seat and, as you go past the marker, either ask your helper to time you between the markers or hit the button on your stopwatch. Pull up gradually afterwards.

Look at the time it took you to cover the 100m as a fraction of one minute. For example, if you took 12 seconds, that is one-fifth of a minute (60 seconds ÷ 12 = 5) so, in a whole minute at that speed, you would travel 5 x 100m, i.e. at 500mpm – faster than necessary at this level.

Do this a few times, adjusting your speed up or down. You may be surprised at how steady and obtainable the required speed really is, as many riders new to eventing who try this usually have to adjust their speed downwards!

Timing and course route information on the start box.

Rider technique

It's important that you and your horse feel comfortable together when galloping across country. Take a leaf out of the race-riders' book and, while cross country schooling or when cantering in the school for fittening work, adopt a position similar to that of a jockey when cantering a horse down to the start of a race. Keep your leg at the girth (not behind it), your seat well out of the saddle, your back long, and the line between your horse's mouth and your elbow straight; so your elbow to your hand is an extension of the rein. The stirrup leathers should hang straight down, with the stirrup on the widest part of the foot. You should be positioned in the middle of the horse and never in front of his movement. In order to adopt this position correctly, it is necessary to ride with leathers shortened several holes compared to flatwork length.

Balance and control

Find your point of balance over the horse's back, and feel that your instep in the stirrup iron has springs. Don't grip in your lower back; feel soft and supple and imagine you have suspension hinges in your hips that can give and take with the movement of the horse.

Try to create a sense of balance. While balancing your *horse* through the reins, *you* need to be balanced on him, without leaning on the reins. If you lose your balance while in your cross country position, use his mane or neckstrap to steady yourself.

You need a rapport through the reins to control your horse while galloping. Don't be too strong or too light; the horse should like the contact, feel it, and respond to it. The feeling you have should be similar to what you would wish for in the hand holding a lunge line when the horse is accepting and cooperative. Don't push your horse constantly with your seat or legs, but encourage him to draw into the contact. You'll know when you have it right when it feels as if he can gallop on forever.

On the approach to a fence, imagine having two-thirds of the horse in front of you and, when jumping fences such as into water or drops, allow the reins to slip through your hands and your lower legs to go forward. When jumping down into water, down steps, or a drop, lean your upper body back, hinging from your hips. This is so that your body is in balance and you are more secure should the horse stumble on landing, or stop. After the fence, go with the horse and move him forward away from the fence.

As the cross country phase is as influential as the dressage and show-jumping, your technique at speed should be practised to the same extent. By starting to practise it slowly, then gradually building up speed, not only will you become a more balanced rider, but you'll soon develop a sense of what is the right cross country speed.

Practise cantering and galloping at speed across all terrains at home before going to an event.

TOP TIPS Better balance

Every rider is a 'rucksack' on their horse's back; it is up to you whether you're balanced or otherwise. Constantly question your position, starting with the base, so equal weight in your stirrups, knees relaxed, sitting equally on both seat bones with your stomach forward and not collapsed inwards. Have equal contact through your elbows to the bit, whether bending your horse or straight. To complete the picture, look straight ahead to where you are going.

> ## TOP TIPS Combining skills
>
> The skill in eventing is not how high you can jump or how much you can teach your horse in the dressage. The important factor is the link between what you are doing in the different disciplines. Whatever you practise in the dressage shouldn't detract from the horse's ability to gallop across country or jump; and what you do in your fittening and jumping work shouldn't prevent your horse executing a good, obedient dressage test.

Downhill confidence

To help improve your balance and confidence, it's important to incorporate hill work. Many riders don't have regular access to acres of undulating countryside so, if most of your riding is done on the flat or in an arena, it's important to find a way of getting experience in riding across undulating country, at first without obstacles. Have a look around for schooling grounds or fun rides with optional fences.

Start off by having a hack around. First, walk up and down a slope or small hill, keeping your horse straight and preferably working as you would in an arena. When you're both confident with that, use a steeper slope and move into trot, rising and standing. Then, shorten up your stirrup leathers and practise your forward (two-point) seat while you canter around. Once you and your horse are both confident and able to remain in balance and the same rhythm, canter up and down the hill. Work towards being able to canter straight up and down and also ride very large circles and ovals. Try to sit, stand and relax as well as work your horse into an outline. It may be useful to ask your coach to help with this when you go cross country schooling.

Once you feel confident and you have practised jumping at home (see Cross Country at Home), you can have a go at jumping a few small fences like logs and roll tops sited on slopes.

With some imagination, hill work can be used to improve your flatwork as well as your general fitness, balance and confidence and help overcome the common fear of riding downhill. Obviously your ability will determine the gradient of slope used.

Natural obstacles are often adapted and used within a cross country course, like this stone wall on a slope.

TOP TIPS Balance and rhythm aid economy

A horse galloping in balance, on a line and in a good rhythm is going to take less out of himself, run less risk of injury, be able to jump better and more economically and therefore save time.

Push-button strides

Take the time to develop an adjustable canter stride for cross-country riding and, once you've discovered these buttons and become familiar with them, you can use them on the course. To practise at home, place two poles on the ground, using between three and four human strides for each horse stride (adjust within this range for your horse or pony's size), then pace out your distance for five reasonably forward, but regular, complete canter strides between the poles. Ride through the poles on five strides, counting the strides out loud and do this a few times from each direction. Then adjust your speed forwards to get four strides, which cover more ground, between the poles, but be sure that the horse is achieving this with hocks still engaged

> ## TOP TIPS Better canter = better jumping
>
> If you can't canter a 10m circle, then it will be very difficult to achieve the right sort of canter and control to jump a coffin. It is all to do with the front and the back end of your horse being connected. So, if you improve your canter generally and your ability to canter that circle, then automatically your jumping will improve.
>
> Opening and closing strides on curved lines is a very good exercise in the school to prepare for the cross country course. And a tip is make sure that you can stand straight up in your stirrups at walk, trot, canter and in transitions when riding at jumping and flat length for balance and strength training.

and is not flat and 'running'. Once you are happy, it is this canter that represents your 'power button', which you can use for tackling ascending spread fences, like a steeplechase fence. Do that a couple of times to get the feel of it, then return to going through on five strides, then add in an extra sixth stride by collecting your horse (shorter strides, but still forward-thinking), and that is your bouncy, coffin canter.

Once you have ridden through the poles a few times and got a good feel for it, practise adjusting the number of strides away from the poles. Also take care that you are not just adjusting with your hand – make sure that your seat and leg are used too.

You can also try to perfect your canter rhythm and adjust your stride length on a circle using two poles. Place a pole on opposite sides of the circle and canter from one pole to the next keeping the same rhythm, counting the strides. Ask you horse to extend for a few strides and then collect. The aim is to keep your horse balanced throughout.

Once you've firmly established your horse's control buttons, your cross country ride will be safer and more fun. Jumping narrow fences, arrowheads, bounces, coffins and spooky fences, like from light into dark, will be so much easier using the coffin canter button. The larger spread fences using the longer, powerful stride will be an exhilarating but confidence-building experience using the power button. As well as having both buttons under your command, you must also have balance, rhythm and control. Your steering, brakes, accelerator and gear changes are now all in place.

Practise bringing your horse forward and back in a steady canter and gallop rhythm.

Cross country at home

Once you are confident of your and your horse's ability to cover undulating ground with balance, rhythm and control and you have established an adjustable canter stride, you can practise your cross country jumping technique by using showjumps and a little imagination.

Techniques like turns after a fence, jumping fences on a curving line, speed of approach to a fence and acceleration after landing can be practised using a few showjumps.

Preparation

Equipment

Ideal equipment for a schooling session would be a couple of sections of solid showjump fillers, plastic drums or showjump wings, a water tray, planks, a brush filler, a couple of small conifer branches for flags and about six poles. If you are using drums, make sure they are secured and cannot roll.

The water tray becomes a ditch, poles either side convert it to a coffin, and so on until you have made every variation possible.

Warming up

Take a bit of time to canter around your arena or field in your warm-up, both sitting down and in your two-point seat. Practise your cross country seat along the long sides of your arena or field, sitting deeper into the seat and collecting on the short side, then increasing speed again along the long side, thus testing your control and brakes.

Warm up over simple obstacles, no matter what your level. A simple fence like a cross-pole is ideal to get you and your horse thinking forward.

Points to practise

Accuracy

Make sure you aim for the centre of your fences, so start off how you mean to go on. Accuracy is a discipline that is really important to stick to, especially as you begin to move up the levels.

How?

Place a few cross-poles around the field or arena, then once you have mastered a single fence on both reins, try the same fence but take it at angles or a curving line. The trick is to increase the angle more and perfect it, as well as increasing the confidence of you and your horse.

Once you are happy, try an off-set double. You need to practise two approaches here. First, take the straight line through, then work on a curving line or dogleg. Typically you will meet these at BE90 and BE100, where you might find a double of logs or roll top fences. The important thing is to keep everything simple, fair and flowing for your horse.

When two courses are running side by side, ensure you have learnt your route so you don't jump the wrong fence!

TOP TIPS **Measuring a stride**

When measuring distances, measure four of your own normal walk strides to one of your horse's strides. Two of your strides is the distance you need either side of a pole to allow for landing or take-off.

TOP TIPS **Distances**

Keep the distances on the short side for an inexperienced horse. So perhaps instead of allowing for eight of your own strides, plus the landing and take-off strides between a two-stride double, measure out seven of your own instead plus the take-off and l anding strides. You will often find this distance used in an indoor arena and it also helps your horse get onto his hocks and prevents a younger or inexperienced horse getting 'strung out'.

Focus your attention on the centre of a fence when jumping a skinny.

Jumping a skinny

You need to focus your eyes and your horse's attention on the centre of the fence. To help do this without the risk of running out, place a pole either side as guide rails.

How?

Start off by placing the secured barrel or filler on its side, then increase the difficulty by making it smaller or putting the barrel on it's end. Approach it in a slow, controlled, bouncy gait. Trot into it to start with if you feel more comfortable.

Keep an even and equal rein contact and your legs close to your horse's side. As you become more confident, you'll find your straightness will improve.

Jumping a corner

Using your poles, barrels or jump wings, make a small corner with a slight angle and jump it at the narrow end. Use a guide pole so that the horse is not tempted to run out.

How?

Jump first near the edge of the corner then, as you get more confident, move down towards the middle, which is where you will want to jump when you are faced with a cross country corner. Don't jump along the front face of the corner; bisect the corner by imagining a spot on the centre of the corner and jump there.

Once you feel happy placing your horse wherever you want him along the length of the corner, you can increase the angle of the poles to make it wider and jump the corner from both directions. Do not try to jump a corner at its widest part, or aim at the decorations on top of a corner, as these are placed to funnel you into the correct position.

Don't jump along the front face of the corner, bisect it by imagining a spot in the centre of the corner and jumping there.

Coaching days

Have two or three cross country schooling lessons before you consider entering a competition. Contact a BE accredited coach in your area: not only will they have expert knowledge, as many of them are professional event riders themselves, but as a BE accredited coach they will be insured and hold a first aid certificate. Some coaches are even based at schooling grounds. To find one, look in the back of the BE *Members' Handbook* or check online at www.britisheventing.com. Three or four lessons are best as, that way, you can plan a series of lessons with specific goals, such as speed, logs, roll tops and forward seat in lesson one; water, rails, hedges, coffin and ditches in lesson two and skinnies, steps, start box and corners in lesson three. As mentioned earlier, expert advice on how to ride up, down and across slopes can also be useful. By lesson four you will be putting it all together and should be happy to set off jumping a course that you and your instructor have strung together in the schooling field. You could also add on half an hour of instruction in the showjumping ring; this way you will be well prepared for your first event!

Top three schooling essentials

You
Drinking water
Gloves, approved hat and BETA Level 3 body protector
Helper or fellow rider with mobile phone

Your horse
Water, bucket and wash down equipment
Neckstrap or martingale
Protective boots

Schooling on a course

Once you have had a few lessons, it is important to try cross country jumping under your own steam. Initially, go to the same schooling venue you have used for your lessons and practise what you have learnt. This will help to build your and your horse's confidence. Then have a look at hiring a local course – lots of BE event courses are open for schooling the day after they have held a BE80(T), BE90 or BE100 event, so check the online schedule, or go to a fun ride where you and your horse can have a canter around a variety of different fences.

TOP TIPS **Schooling safely**

When you go cross country schooling, take a helper with you, or go
with a fellow rider and make sure you both have mobile phones in
case of an accident. Have the phone number of the schooling venue
saved into your phone in case your horse gets away from you so
that you can call ahead to warn them he may be arriving loose into
the yard! If you don't have a helper or friend available, make sure
you tell the venue manager you are alone so they can keep an eye
out for you, or buddy yourself up with others using the course.

TOP TIPS **Substitute neckstrap**

If you don't ride with a martingale or have a neckstrap, use a spare
stirrup leather and buckle it up as a neckstrap on your horse.
This will give you extra security to grab onto if your horse's mane
is short or if you suddenly need to regain your balance – if, for
instance, your horse trips in the water or stumbles on approach to a
fence. It also is a great balancing aid that won't interfere with your
horse's mouth as the reins would if you suddenly needed to grab it.

Warming up

Whenever you go to a schooling field, canter around the perimeter, taking
note of where certain fences are that you want to jump. For example, take
note of a roll top, rails, ditch, coffin, bench, brush fence, steps, water and a
small log. Also have a look out for a suitable corner and a skinny fence. As
you make your way around the field, go up and down the gears both in trot,
canter and gallop for a good ten minutes.

Practise your forward seat (see page 128). If you need to, now is the time to
shorten your stirrup leathers and tighten your girth. Once you've done this,
find an area near a small fence, like a log and work your horse in a large circle.
Send him forward from the leg, bringing him back, circling and spiralling in
and out, making sure he is listening to your leg aids. Practise your bouncy,
coffin canter and power canter. Once you feel confident that he is attentive,

When you arrive at the cross country schooling ground, trot or canter around the fences, planning which fences you are going to jump and in which order.

work the log into your warm-up, first jumping it directly in the middle and then on both sides, then from a slight angle from both sides. Once you are both happy and confident, work in a couple of other small fences, jumping them individually.

- Don't be afraid of jumping around in a slower, more comfortable rhythm. That way you'll take fewer pulls before a fence, which can unsettle your horse and disturb your rhythm. It can also save time as you don't have to do too much setting up for the fence.

- Always go cross country in a breastplate, martingale or neckstrap so you have some extra security if you need it.

- Practise your ability to change gear in order to approach different types of fences at the right speed and stride length. Remember that it is you, the rider, who is responsible for the correct gear and line.

- Learn to judge speed by using your watch's minute hand or a stopwatch. Measure out a distance, and then time yourself cantering along that line.

- Perfect your position. You should be out of the saddle in a two-point seat between fences and then change to come closer to the saddle, or sitting, when approaching a fence, three or four strides out.

- Looking at the fence as a whole, and looking beyond the fence, will assist you in choosing the correct line through and then away from that fence to the next obstacle.

When jumping in water, make sure you can slip your reins if your horse stumbles.

Jumping a course

Once you have jumped say four or five fences, take a breather, walking your horse around while you work out how to string those fences together as a mini course. Once you are happy with the order in which you are going to jump them, circle your horse around in canter a couple of times, then set off confidently on your course. Once you have completed it, do it again, then move to another part of the schooling field and start jumping some different fences individually again before stringing them together as a course. If you have a problem, bring it right back to basics and practise over the small log again.

Key fences

On your initial canter around the field, you will have noted key fences that you need to jump such as a small ditch, rails, brush fence, steps, water, roll top, coffin, bench, corner and skinny. These are typical fences that you will find on a BE course up to BE100 level. Not all of these will be included on a BE80(T) or BE90 course, but it is worth practising them so that when you get to your first event, you will feel confident about jumping what you see on the course. Some courses also have a start box for you to practise your start, so make the most of it!

Spread fences are common on cross country courses.

OPPOSITE Start off your practice by jumping a simple log to get you both thinking forward.

TOP TIPS Different approaches

▶ **Sloping fences** with a good ground line, like a steeplechase fence, can be jumped out of your horse's galloping stride or a forward-going canter and shouldn't need too much setting up.

▼ **Single fences** with an upright front like a gate or rail needs a certain amount of precision, so you need to set up and approach at a steadier, more controlled canter.

▼ **For steps** up you need to change down a gear to create a rounder, bouncier canter so as to approach them on a slightly accelerating stride to give you the required momentum to get up them.

▼ **For drops**, combinations or water you must change down a couple of gears to go slowly enough for the horse to see what is there, figure out what to do and then do it, but still create enough forward impulsion so that he will take on the obstacle.

Water

Next, find the water and walk your horse through several times from different angles. Stop in the middle and let him reach down and splash about. Then walk around in large circles so he can get used to the feel. Next, move on to trotting him gently into and out of the water, making sure that your reins are long and loose in your fingers, just in case he trips. Some schooling fields have small logs or steps on the entrance to or exit from the water, or

a few strides away from the water's edge. If you're both enjoying it and feel confident, have a go at trotting through the water then popping over the log on the exit. At BE80(T) and BE90 level, you are not expected to jump into or out of the water, but some BE100 courses do have a small step in or a log a couple of strides from the edge of the water, so it's important to practise what you may encounter on a course.

Useful experience and knowledge

The more relevant experience you have, and the more you know about what will be involved, the better you will be prepared for your first event.

Ringcraft

Before you enter your first event, as well as doing all your schooling, make sure you have been to a few local competitions so that both you and your horse get the feel of a competition atmosphere. It's amazing how even the quietest of horses can become fizzy once the ramp drops and they see the other horses and hear the tannoy!

Having fun at a few low-level competitions is also a great way to combat any competition nerves you may have! (Check out the section on Sports Psychology on page 90). Don't put any pressure on yourself to win, just go along to soak up the atmosphere, for the experience and, most importantly, the fun.

Your confidence, and ultimately your ringcraft, will improve the more events you do.

TOP TIPS **Preparation checklist**

Before you enter an event make sure you have:

- Had a few cross country lessons.

- Gone cross country schooling.

- Practised a variety of cross country fences relevant to your level.

- Gone to a couple of dressage and showjumping competitions.

OPPOSITE Once you have walked through the water, try trotting and cantering through it.

Understanding course design

The importance of good course design has never been higher and a full understanding of what it's all about is essential, if the resulting course is going to be 'good' from the viewpoint of the course designer, the organiser and the riders. Understanding what the course designer has in mind is very important to your assessment of how to ride the course.

Course design involves so much more than just scattering a random series of obstacles across a number of fields. Good courses need careful planning and a designer who has a good 'feel' for the job and an understanding of what the fundamental requirements are.

Boat or barge portable fences are popular at water complexes.

A course needs to have a 'flow' to it; there must be a balance to where the questions are asked, and there must be a reason, however simple, for every single fence on a course, whether it be a 'let up' fence, or simply a question of whether the rider can actually ride a turn, a drop, an uphill fence or a combination.

So, what goes into a good cross country course and what can you expect to meet?

At the introductory levels it's all about education and fun rather than examination or testing. All horses and riders should be expected to jump a variety of different types of fences, albeit straightforward ones. A course should give horses and riders the opportunity to gain confidence and learn from the experience. It's important that horses and riders are introduced to the types of fences that they can expect to meet higher up the levels, but in a much simpler form and situation. Some of the fences perceived to be more 'difficult' may have an alternative for the less experienced, the thinking being that everyone should have the opportunity to get round the course.

At the introductory levels, time shouldn't be something to worry about. There's a feeling that because a competition is under BE rules there's a need to go fast – nothing could be further from the truth. The speed required is very generous, but it's certainly worth going out and learning what riding at 450mpm feels like.

Clearly, as the levels progress, so the expectations placed upon riders and horses change. You'll be expected to have more experience and so be able to jump at a progressively higher speed. The fences become a little bigger and more sophisticated, but all the time there has to be an active thought process in the mind of the course designer and builder that horses and riders are always learning, and there's always another competition to go to.

Horses need to have their confidence kept intact, and riders need to feel confident that if they enter an event they'll get a good course with no tricks and have a good experience.

Introductory course questions

- Trakehners or open ditches (post and rails or palisades with a ditch in front) where the 'ditch' can be as simple as a scoop in the ground just to create the idea.

- Narrow fences framed using Christmas trees or similar to give horses and riders the feel of jumping a narrow fence (not really 'skinnies' but they begin the thought process and they must be such that horses are encouraged to jump them as opposed to running out).

- Simple, small drop fences.

- Simple uphill fences.

- Simple spreads and corners.

- Straightforward combinations with plenty of width of fence and also appropriate distances between elements.

- Straightforward turning questions.

- Simple water obstacles which offer a run in and out rather than a jump landing into water, and the water must be shallow in order to give a good experience.

A simple trakehner fence.

10

THE EVENT

Here you'll find everything you'll need to know about what actually happens on the day of your event, from the last-minute essential preparations the day before leaving the yard, to what to do on arrival at the event when getting yourself geared up for the day.

Dress and equipment

In your preparation it is important to know just what you and your horse need to wear – not just the right equipment for each phase, but for safety.

The table overleaf gives a summary of the main points of rider wear, but you are advised to check in the *Member's Handbook* for further clarification.

The situation regarding horse wear is more complex than that for the rider – there are potentially more items and patterns of equipment that a horse might conceivably wear; some may be permissible at certain stages only; and rules are modified on occasion, either to accommodate or prohibit new items as they come into popular use. Best advice, is, therefore, to check a *current Member's Handbook* or call the Sport Team on 0845 262 3344 for all points of detail regarding equipment for the horse. Take care regarding this matter, bearing in mind that *you* are ultimately responsible for your horse wearing permissible equipment.

Rider wear

Dressage
(BE80(T), BE90, BE100, BE100 Plus)

- Protective headwear, dark blue or black in colour.
- Black or dark blue coat with white stock or tweed coat with coloured stock or collar and tie.
- Gloves.
- Buff/fawn breeches.
- Plain black or brown boots, leather gaiters with matching boots (not half chaps).
- Service uniform.

Showjumping

- Protective headwear, dark blue or black in colour.
- Black or dark blue coat with white stock or tweed coat with coloured stock or collar and tie.
- Gloves.
- Buff/fawn breeches.
- Plain black or brown boots, leather gaiters with matching boots (not half chaps)
- Service uniform.

Cross country

- Protective headwear with cover.
- Cross country colours.
- White, buff or fawn breeches.
- Plain black or brown boots, leather gaiters with matching boots (not half chaps).
- Level 3 body protector.
- Gloves.

General
Protective headwear (hats)

A 'riding hat' must be worn at all times by anyone, whether or not a competitor, riding anywhere at a BE event. It must conform to current safety standards, which are updated periodically, so check the BE website to ensure that your hat, and that of anyone else riding your horse, is an acceptable model. The hat harness of anyone riding at the event must be correctly fastened.

A competitor's hat must show a visible BE 'hat tag', which can be affixed at the secretary's tent on inspection to show that it conforms to current safety standards.

Competitors are strongly recommended to check their hats regularly and replace them if damaged, or following a fall.

Whips

No whip of any kind may be carried while competing in the dressage test. A whip no longer than 120cm including lash may be carried when riding on the flat at any other time.

One whip, no longer than 75cm and not weighted, may be carried when jumping any obstacle.

Jewellery

Jewellery worn anywhere on the body can increase the risk of injury. Competitors are strongly recommended to remove all jewellery, especially before the jumping phases.

Hair

In the interests of safety long hair should be secured appropriately.

OPPOSITE Long hair should be secured in a bun or ponytail in a hairnet.

EVENT GROOM'S TIPS Attention to detail

- Be organised and one step ahead of the game all of the time. Get ready in plenty of time, then you know you have time to spare if something goes wrong.

- It's important to maintain your horse's mane; you can't get beautiful plaits from a messy mane. It makes a difference to see a nicely trimmed tail and heels to help define your horse so make sure you do all trimming prior to the day. Wash your horse's mane three days prior to plaiting. Once washed, band it over so that it lies correctly.

- Turnout in eventing doesn't win you any points, but it helps to create a professional picture. Make sure you're tidy as well, to add the finishing touches.

- Look after your stud kit. Clean the studs after each use and keep the different studs separate. It sounds basic but it really helps to speed things up on the day. Clean out stud holes the day before; tap them and pack them with cotton or natural wool so that, on the day, you can just pick the wool out and put the studs in. Once you've finished, take the studs out as soon as ➤

you can – don't have the horse wandering around with studs and no boots in case of injuries.

- When it comes to quarter markings they look very smart if they're done properly, but make sure you practise at home as badly done quarter marks can spoil the picture.

- Clean your tack before the day and have it all set out ready for each phase. Stick a plaiting needle, or buckle end, through the punched holes to remove any remnants of saddle soap. Polished buckles give the finishing touch.

- If you are travelling a long way then allow enough time for your horse to get his head down and pick at some grass once you arrive. This helps to drain the airways.

- Have someone down at the dressage to help you take boots off, hold your whip, make sure your number is straight, and keep an eye on your arena so you can concentrate on riding.

- When cooling down after the cross country have five or six buckets ready for when you return. If it's a hot day put ice in and keep your horse in the shade. If he's still blowing when he comes back, get a few buckets over him, sweat-scrape and then walk him purposefully, then get a few more buckets, scrape and walk until he has stopped blowing.

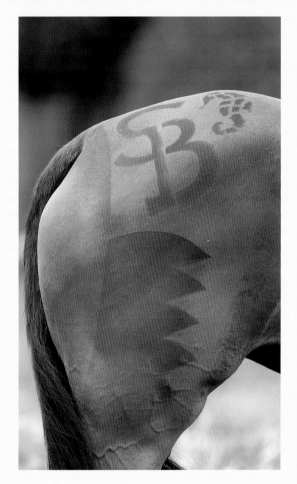

Quarter markings look great.

- Know your horse's legs and hooves. Check them every day; even though he comes back sound from the cross country, it's important to check that he's still sound in the morning and that there's no heat or swelling. If you do find heat or swelling, ice for twenty minutes, monitor and call your vet for advice.

- If you're at an event for the whole day, get your horse off the box and offer him water and a pick of grass.

The week before the event

What to do in case of problems

Withdrawing

If you need to withdraw for any reason, check the schedule to see who it is you need to contact. You may get a partial refund if your space is filled – all those details are event-specific and can be found in the schedule. You may need to show a veterinary certificate to get your refund, so ask your vet for one if you have had to call him out. (This doesn't apply to a doctor's certificate if you are unfit yourself, the reasoning being that you may be able to ask another BE member to ride your horse for you.)

Remember to cancel your stabling if you have booked this, too.

Event cancellations

It is very rare for an event to cancel, but if it happens it is usually to do with the weather. Organisers do not take the decision lightly, and it is only after course inspections and discussions with the technical adviser and steward that they can agree to cancel for safety reasons. As well as the requirement for horses can get around as safely as possible, it is essential that ambulances can get to all areas of the course without getting stuck.

If the UK is experiencing exceptionally wet weather and flooding, and several events are cancelled, some may be able to postpone to another time, but it all depends on the Eventing Calendar, as a new date could adversely affect other local events which are scheduled to run. Check the BE website or call your regional coordinator for advice.

If an event cancels, you are entitled to a refund. Check the BE *Members' Handbook* for details.

An event can also be abandoned once it is running if the conditions deteriorate and it is deemed dangerous to continue. Again, check the BE *Members' Handbook*.

Schooling and horse care

Check that you've learnt the correct dressage test (so you don't have that sinking feeling when you watch the competitor before you turn left instead of right after the centre line!).

Ensure your trailer or lorry is ready for the road.

It's worth running through the test a few times at home or with your coach to familiarise yourself with the test and the movements, but not so many times that your horse learns it too and starts to anticipate turns and changes of gait!

It's important that you and your horse arrive fresh and ready for the event, so don't try to cram lessons, jump training and other competitions in the week before (see Horse Fitness page 47).

Check your horse's legs twice a day, every day, including an inspection of his shoes, particularly after riding.

Transport

Ensure that your trailer or lorry is ready for the road. Fill up your lorry (or towing vehicle) with fuel, check that the plating, insurance and road tax are up to date, pack your kit and food and take the vehicle on a couple of short runs to ensure it is driving (and importantly, starting) well. Check all the tyres, lights and ramps on your lorry or trailer.

EVENT GROOM'S TIPS The week before

- Well in advance, make sure you've got all the kit you'll need and that everything is washed, mended and fits. If it's your first event with that particular horse make sure you've used all your competition tack at home at least a couple of times before the big day.

- It can be handy to have a smaller separate grooming kit for shows. It also means that you can keep it in the horsebox or trailer so it's one less thing to pack the day before. You only need the essential grooming tools plus a few lotions and potions!

- A few days before the competition make sure that manes and tails are pulled and feathers are trimmed. Pull manes and tails using latex gloves; they give you more grip and it's a lot quicker than the comb method. Ideally, manes should be washed now as otherwise, if they are too silky, they can be harder to plait.

Clean your tack well and check for wear and tear.

If it is your first competition and it is quite a distance away from home, it may be better to stay overnight. You can book stabling at the same time as making your entry.

Making a timetable

Make up a timetable for the day of the competition and give a copy to whoever is helping you, or stick it to the door of your tack locker.

Include things like:

- Time of arrival, time of working-in for the dressage, your actual dressage time – with the arena number if applicable.

- When you intend to fetch your horse to work him in for your showjumping round, your actual showjumping time – note also your change of equipment, boots, etc.

- Time to get warmed-up for the cross country, your actual cross country time, equipment list.

- Remember you also need to allow time to move between each phase, change your clothes and your horse's tack, boots and studs.

Don't forget the detail!

Get your packing and equipment lists ready, double-check your horse's vaccination certificate and passport and fill in your medical card. Remember to phone or check online for your start times so you can add them to your timetable. Ensure you have directions to the event and estimate how long it will take to get there, including any possible hold-ups.

Check that your hat and body protector are within BE's guidelines (see pages 213–4).

Note your times in a prominent place.

The day before the event

If the competition is local, you may want to drive over and have a look around the site and do your first course-walk. Double-check that all your equipment is safe and that your tack is clean and within the rules of the competition. (See Dress and Equipment on page 151–2 or check the BE website. Sort out your own clothes and pop them on hangers for each phase. Check your medical card and your number bib.

If you are leaving early the following morning, plait your horse and put him in a clean, grease-free rug – especially valid if you have a grey! (Although plaiting is not compulsory, it looks neat and tidy on the day and can also highlight your horse's conformation. For a long neck have fewer, but bigger plaits; for a short neck, have more, smaller plaits.) Clean out and pack his stud holes, if you have them.

Ideally, plait up the day before.

EVENT GROOM'S TIPS **Rider turnout**

- To avoid getting black polish boot marks on your white saddle cloth, use a neutral coloured polish on the top of the boots.

- To keep a shine on your boots, spray on a light mist of hair spray.

- To help a velvet riding hat look like new, boil a kettle and hold the hat over the steam. Use a soft brush to brush your hat gently and remove any dust. For stubborn stains, use a damp sponge in the same direction as the fibres.

Horse and rider beautifully turned out for dressage.

DIETARY TIPS Eating the day before

Planning your competition day diet should begin, in most cases, the day before and particularly with the last meal of the day. If you are riding very early in the morning, this may be the last time you can top up your muscle glycogen stores.

The meal should only contain familiar foods, with plenty of carbohydrates. However, reduce the amount of fibre-rich sources of carbohydrate, which may cause tummy problems.

Your fluid intake should be maintained at a high level – especially important if you find eating difficult on competition day.

What to pack

Snacks

Fresh or tinned fruit

Packets of dried fruit and nuts

Cartons of low-fat custard, rice pudding or jellies

Cereal bars

Breakfast cereals (can be eaten day and night with or without milk)

Bread sticks, pretzels, crackers, rice cakes, crispbreads

Malt loaf, pancakes, scones, fig rolls and Jaffa Cakes

Spreads, such as jam, honey, peanut butter

Bread rolls or bagels

Drinks

Water

Cartons of long-life fruit juice

Low-sugar cordial

Isotonic sports drinks, in bottles or as a powder

UHT low-fat milk shakes

Checklist for the day

Write out an equipment checklist, working from head to toe (for both you and your horse!). Tick things off when you load up the vehicle so you know that when you arrive at the competition, you'll not be without a vital piece of equipment.

Nerves can often make a rider appear to be disorganised and anxious on the day, but by being confident that everything is in its place and ready, you can focus fully on mentally rehearsing the following day's good performance.

> **TOP TIPS Dirty tack**
>
> Add to your list a couple of bin bags in which to put your horse's wet dirty boots, numnahs, etc. as you untack. Not only is it then easy to take them out and wash them when you get home; it also doesn't dirty your clean equipment. Do the same with your own clothes.

If you are stabling away overnight, ensure you take your skipping out equipment.

Equipment Checklist

Horse	Rider	General
Bridle/s	Hats	Full water container
Saddle/s	Stock/tie & pin	Buckets
Girth/s	Shirt	Sponges
Studs	Breeches or jodhpurs	Feed
Stud tap	Boots	Hay/haylage and haynets
Irons and leathers	Spurs – not compulsory	Skip and tools
Numnahs	Cross country colours	First aid kit – human
Breastplate/girth	Jacket	First aid kit – horse
Martingale	Number bib	Plaiting kit
Headcollar and rope (plus spare)	Medical card and armband	Food and drink
Overreach boots	Gloves	BE *Members' Handbook*
Boots (showjumping and cross country)	Body protector, Level 3	*British Eventing Life* Magazine
Grooming kit, including event grease, if using	Course-walking footwear and spare clothes	Map
Cooler rug	Whip	Wet weather gear and/or sun cream
Travelling rugs, boots, tail guard		Confirmation letter
Night rugs (if staying away)		Start fee(s)
Vaccination certificate		Fly spray
Passport (under Defra rules it is illegal to transport horses without a valid passport)		Spare set of horse shoes

Regularly check all equipment and tack and ensure it is all safe, in good condition and fits correctly.

DIETARY TIPS Pre-competition meal

Eat two to four hours before the event as this allows time for your meal to empty from your stomach (so four hours for a larger meal). Fill up but don't overeat. Eat a comfortable amount of food and keep the fat content down as that will slow digestion. Go for a moderate amount of protein and fill up on carbohydrates instead, for maximum energy.

Or, if you are nervous and can't eat, drink your meal, like a sports drink or milk shake.

Some riders like a snack half an hour to an hour before warming up, which can help as long as enough carbohydrate is eaten. Try to drink at least 200ml of fluid just before warming up.

VETERINARY TIPS Travelling

Ensure your horse arrives at the event in a state to compete by paying particular attention to his travelling conditions.

- Make sure there's good ventilation in the lorry or trailer. Don't over-rug him as he should be kept cool rather than warm. Sweat and electrolyte loss occur during travel, both to and from an event.

- Correctly fitted travel boots or bandages will help to protect your horse's legs, so make sure you have your travel kit ready for the journey. Also make sure the box or trailer is safe and well maintained.

- Your horse should have free access to water prior to travelling so that he's fully hydrated. Give him sufficient time to drink before travelling, especially if you've a long journey ahead. Transporting a dehydrated horse can lead to problems such as colic or shipping sickness (pleuropneumonia). You should always have an equine thermometer in your first aid kit in the vehicle to monitor his temperature, especially after a long journey.

EVENT GROOM'S TIPS Competition day

This can mean a really early start but always be on the yard in plenty of time to feed and let your horse digest his breakfast before putting him on the lorry. You might find you need to re-wash his legs and remove any stable stains.

On competition day you want your horse to be shining so, to combat scurf, give the horse a good brush to lift the grease then get a bucket of hot water and add a few squirts of baby oil. Use a well wrung out towel to rub all over in big circular motions, paying extra attention to the quarters, and your horse will be gleaming.

Keep your baby wipes handy for any stable stains if you have a grey.

Before you leave the yard...

Before setting off for the event, check that all is well with your horse. Check he has eaten his food and has drunk. Trot him out in hand to make sure he is sound and has four shoes.

If you have stud holes, double-check that the studs are still packed. Leave in plenty of time to allow for traffic hold-ups on the way and any queues into the lorry park. You should arrive at least an hour before you intend to get on you horse for the first phase, but that will all depend on whether you intend to walk the showjumping and cross country courses before or after your dressage.

Bandage your horse's tail to protect it before travelling, and take it off just before the dressage.

Have your plan of what you are going to do on the day and stick to it, so that you get to all the phases with plenty of time to spare.

Competition day

Control the day by your use of forward planning, preparation and attention to detail. Calm any nerves with the knowledge that you have prepared your horse and yourself to the maximum of your ability. Give yourself plenty of time to prepare for each phase and keep warm; nerves get worse when you are cold. Everyone gets a touch of butterflies, so relax and enjoy the day; remember – you do this for fun!

On arrival

Your horse

On arrival, check that your horse has travelled OK and look him over in the lorry or trailer for any bumps. Take off his travel boots and bandages, give him some extra room in the partition and open up the windows to the horse area so he can get some fresh air. Depending on what time your dressage is, consider giving him a bite of fodder and offer him some water. This is something you might like to ask one of your helpers to do while you go over to the secretary's tent to declare your entry.

Tacked up and ready for action!

You

When going out of the horsebox park, make a mental note of which direction the riders are going for the various phases – this may save time later!

Remember to take your horse's vaccination certificate and passport to the secretary's tent. Here, you'll collect your number, pay your start fee (have the right money as they aren't banks!), double-check your times, and ensure that the event is running to time (this is something that is worth checking throughout the day, but it's normally announced if there are any delays). Get your hat tagged if this is your first event or you have bought a new hat.

If your plan was to walk the course again, make sure the markers are set for your class and that there haven't been any alterations; this is particularly relevant if you are on the second or even third day for your level of class. On returning to your box, lay everything out for each phase, prepare the water, get dressed for the first phase and put your studs in ready.

EVENT GROOM'S TIPS At the event

If you get to the competition and there's mud everywhere, spray a light layer of mane and tail spray onto your horse's fetlock and pastern area below the warm-up boots or bandages. Then, just before you enter the dressage arena, ask your helper to run a baby wipe over the horse's lower legs. The moisture binds with the mane and tail spray and removes any wet, horrid mud cleanly and swiftly. Baby wipes are an essential item in your grooming kit and can also be used for cleaning noses, eyes and docks as well as removing any stains once at the competition.

For that finishing touch on black hooves, use black boot polish and then add a layer of clear hoof oil on top. This keeps them looking black and shiny.

VETERINARY TIPS Care of your horse at the event

On arrival, unload your horse and let him lower his head to help drain any mucus from his airways, perhaps by giving him a pick of grass, then walk him around. Check him over for any injuries he may have sustained on the journey.

During the day, make sure he has regular access to water, and provide feed or hay at appropriate times according to your competition schedule. Check him over after each phase for any minor injuries or knocks and check that his shoes and the nails are all in place.

Cross country course-walk

Walking the course is an art and should be taken seriously – almost as a phase
in itself. If possible, walk the cross country course the day before the event.
Go to the secretary's tent, where there will be a plan of the course. Check
the number of fences and the time allowed (although time should not be the
ultimate factor in your preparation at this stage). If in doubt you will find the
optimum time on the start box. Try to walk the course three times. The first

Try to walk the cross
country course three
times.

walk will be as if in your horse's shoes – first impressions count, because that is how he will view the course. Your first view of each obstacle has to relate to your horse, his ability and his thinking.

The second walk is for you! Study the ground, the approach, the position of the fence and any alternative routes. Choose your line to each fence. Consider carefully the best route and look out for where the sun might be shining or where excessive shade may fall, depending on the time of day of your run. If you are walking the course the day beforehand, try to do so at the same time as when you will ride it, as theoretically the sun will be in the same position – a good plan, but not always the case owing to our great British weather! Perhaps also consider how you will cope and what you will do if the take-offs and landings become poached after fifty or more horses have run, so don't just look at lines to the middle of the fences; perhaps consider what your line might be like if you jumped nearer one of the marker flags – although, that said, the footing at an affiliated event is well maintained by the on-site fence repair team.

Check very, very carefully for flags, coloured markers and any messages stapled to the fences. Be absolutely precise about your route at combinations, angles and anywhere there may be the slightest chance you might cross your tracks. Some combination fences are numbered separately; others are labelled as A and B elements. With the latter, you mustn't ride a circle between them or cross your tracks, or you will be penalised. If they are numbered separately, you are permitted to circle between or around them without penalty provided you have not already presented your horse at the element. This is particularly relevant where combinations may be numbered individually or where there are several routes into a water obstacle.

When you walk the course, consider if part of it may be in shade when it is time for you to ride.

Walk your line

As you approach each fence, stop about twelve horse's strides away from the fence, look behind you to see where you have walked, look through the flags of the fence in front of you and get your eye into a line at a point in the distance. Walk towards and over the fence with your eye on your chosen point.

The course should be walked in that manner from start box to finish flags. Your line point in the distance may be a marker to turn by; it may be the next fence, or anything obvious and immovable, but get into this habit so that when you jump the fence, your head is up and you can power to the next obstacle, using your line.

When checking your line, take the time to stop and look behind you, study carefully the line that you have just walked, then look forward at the line and angle you are walking to the next fence. Imagine a line of dots that you are joining up.

The third walk should be full of motivation and confidence. You know where you are going, you are aware of the uneven bits of ground, every tree stump, rocks and low branches. The course should look so much easier on your third trip round.

When you walk your line around the course, remember to look out for overhanging branches that may hamper your round.

DIETARY TIPS **Think drink!**

Up to 65 per cent of a rider's body is water and this needs to be maintained for health and sporting performance. When riding, your body produces heat, and fluid is lost as sweat to help reduce your body temperature. This fluid needs to be replaced, as even a small amount of dehydration can result in a dramatic loss of performance.

Dehydration will affect your strength, endurance, coordination, concentration and visual accuracy.

Thirst is a poor indication of dehydration, as by the time you are thirsty you are already dehydrated. Other symptoms include dark urine, headaches, irritability, weakness, dizziness and cramp.

Fluid must be consumed at regular intervals during the day to replace ongoing losses. Most people need to drink 2 litres a day plus extra when riding or if the weather is hot.

Avoid fizzy drinks as they can cause bloating.

Remember to drink between phases.

Working-in tips – what horse have you?

You may have already worked out an ideal working-in time and routine for your horse. If not, check below to see if you can recognise your horse's personality, as it may help you to plan.

Excitable horse

An early quiet start time is best. When making your entry, you can make such a request and the secretary will do their best to accommodate you – although it is not always possible. Keep your horse as calm as possible,

Keep a laid-back horse interested and active, so less working-in time and sharper transitions.

go to have your tack checked by the steward as soon as you arrive in the collecting area. Ride your horse in as close to your arena as you are allowed. Slow all the gaits down, to a rhythmical slow beat with gentle sweeping changes of rein, progressive, quiet transactions. Plenty of walk work.

Nervous horse

It is sometimes helpful to allow extra time to walk the horse in hand in the dressage area and let him nibble a little grass, before taking him back to the lorry to tack up. Keep speaking to your horse – plenty of pats and reassurance.

Inattentive horse

This type requires a different approach: you must keep his mind on you. Still keep everything calm, with forward rhythm, straight with impulsion. Ride many changes of rein and plenty of transitions to keep his attention on you and what you are going to ask next.

Laid-back horse

Any dressage time will suit you. The trick with this horse will be to keep him interested and active, so less working-in time and sharper (direct) transitions now and again, e.g. halt to trot, walk to canter. He might even benefit from jumping a cross-pole before going to the dressage area. Work him in different parts of the collecting area, going close to the dressage arena just before his test.

TOP TIPS Warm-up essentials

- When riding in the warm-up area, keep away from other horses – you'll need to think ahead to avoid any close encounters!

- Three horses before your test, stand quietly looking at the arena, going over the test in your mind as though you were actually riding it.

- Two horses to go, start to work again and concentrate on keeping your horse listening to you; maintain this until the end of your own test.

> **TOP TIPS Dressage helper's checklist**
>
> Rule book
>
> Boots and whip fine in the warm-up – NOT in the test!
>
> Fly repellent
>
> Copy of the test
>
> Horse rug in case of a hold-up

> **TOP TIPS Dressage start time**
>
> You must be ready to start on your own allotted time, but if your arena is running ahead of schedule don't feel pressured to go early if you are not ready – the choice is yours.

The dressage

The warm-up area can get packed if it's a full section, so it is wise to leave it to just competitors and trainers. Therefore please ask your helpers to stay by the tapes for their own safety.

It's your responsibility to declare your intention to compete to the relevant steward. Each steward wears a letter depicting which section they are running, so it is easier for you or your helper to pinpoint the right person! The steward will then tick your number off their list and tell you which arena you will be in, also whether the arenas are running to time and how many competitors are before you. They can also tell you which number you'll follow, so if you keep an eye on that competitor in the collecting ring you'll be better aware of your time to go forward to the test arena.

Remember to find your steward as soon as you get to the practice area! If you are taking part in a BE80(T) section, you will also be able to find out who and where the allocated trainers are if you want to speak with them or ask them for any help with your warm-up.

Once the steward calls you forward for your test, thank them for their help and then walk courteously past the other dressage arenas so as not to

Find the steward
monitoring your
dressage section.

spook the other horses. Once you have reached your arena, ride around the outside of the arena (*not through it*) to the judge and their writer who will be sitting in their car positioned just behind the centre line at C. Speak, smile or just make eye contact with them, so they know you are ready to start and they can tell you if they have any problems with timings or the arena.

When you ride around the arena, look up, ride your lines and concentrate on getting your horse going forward in a good rhythm. You have forty-five seconds from the sounding of the bell or horn by the judge in which to enter the arena, so don't rush in at A as soon as you hear the bell if you are not entirely confident that you are ready.

Once you have done your test and performed your salute to the judge, remember to smile and reassure your horse with a pat. Leave the arena at A at a walk on a loose rein and walk courteously and quietly past the other arenas.

OPPOSITE From time to
time the overall event
steward will observe how
the phases are running.

Dressage penalties

(BE100 and below)

Compulsory elimination

- Three errors of course (1st error incurs 2 penalties; 2nd error a further 4; 3rd error means elimination)

- Resistance exceeding twenty seconds

- Horse leaving arena with all four feet, if the arena has a continuous surround higher than 23cm

- Leaving arena when out of control

- Marked lameness

- Carrying a whip

- Horse wearing boots or bandages

- Outside assistance

Discretionary elimination

- At the discretion of the BE steward or judge, a competitor can be eliminated for:

- Entering the arena before the starting signal

- Failure to enter arena within forty-five seconds of the start signal

- Riding the wrong test

- Failure to observe dress rules

The above are only a selection of the Rules. For current Rules, check the BE Members' Handbook beforehand and take it with you to all events.

TOP TIPS Dressage divas

Often when you get to the warm-up area, you'll see riders practising their lengthened strides. Don't worry!

Take fifteen or twenty minutes just walking around the warm-up area and as much of the competition area as you can, letting your horse relax, take in the sights and loosen off after travelling.

A stiff, tense horse will not settle down to work and as you may be a little anxious too, make the most of this 'chill time' and build it into your timing plan.

Between phases

Walk the distance between combinations.

The amount of time you have between the phases will depict the pattern of the day for you. Either you will have already walked both the cross country and the showjumping if your phase times are close together, or you will walk the separate phases in-between. Whatever you decide to do, allow yourself enough time! It usually takes an hour to walk a cross country course once, so make sure you have time to do it a couple of times.

Dressage test over, walk quietly back to the lorry, letting your girths down a couple of holes. Untack, let your horse relax, and offer him a drink. Depending on your running times you might give him a small feed, but do remember he must have at least two hours after a feed before any strenuous exercise, and even then only a small feed should be given. Put all your dressage equipment away that is not needed again and get ready for the showjumping.

The showjumping

Check your list to ensure you have everything you need like studs, open-fronted tendon boots, rear boots if used, shorten your stirrup leathers, grab your stick, gloves, hat, change of tack, put on your martingale or breastplate and get your helper to bring along a rug to the collecting ring.

When warming up, riders usually start off with a cross-pole or small upright to get their horses thinking forward. Your job will be to jump enough fences to get your horse thinking forward but not so many that he starts to become jaded, bored or careless. Only you know your horse, so be guided by how you both feel on the day. As a general rule, try a couple of cross-poles, an upright or two then finish with a spread on a good note. See the simple Showjump Warm-up Routine on page 181 for more tips.

Once called forward, slip into the arena alongside the tapes so as not to disturb the previous competitor's round. Once they have finished and come through the finish timers, move off briskly and positively, perhaps ride a circle, taking care not to go through the starting timers until the bell has sounded. You have forty-five seconds from when the bell rings to start your round.

You may need to change your studs for each phase.

TOP TIPS Practice arena etiquette

If your helpers are changing the fences for you, make sure that when they are about to alter them, there isn't a rider already on their approach! This sounds simple but it can very often happen when the ring is busy!

Remember to be courteous to other riders' needs and do not hog the practice fence! Your helpers must also put the fence back to a cross-pole once you have jumped it as an upright, so other riders without helpers can start their warm-up.

Showjumping penalties

(BE100 and below)

- Knockdown – 4 penalties

- First refusal/disobedience – 4 penalties

- Second refusal/disobedience – 8 penalties

- Third refusal/disobedience – elimination

- First fall of rider – 8 penalties

- Second fall of rider – elimination

- Error of course not rectified – elimination

- First fall of horse – elimination

- For every second in excess of the time allowed – 1 penalty

- Exceeding the time limit (which is twice the time allowed) – elimination

- Exceeding 25 penalties (not including time) – compulsory retirement

The above are only a selection of the Rules. For all current Rules, check the BE Members' Handbook beforehand and take it with you to all events.

Simple showjump warm-up routine

Get your horse out at least thirty minutes before your time. Walk, but move him about purposefully. Leg-yield on each side, then ride forward and straight, ride him between your hand and leg and make him pay attention to you. Do the same in trot. When in canter, rhythm is all-important but still have the horse between hand and leg. Shorten and lengthen the stride but do not lose the rhythm.

At the practice fence, keep your wits about you! Look ahead and don't wander into any other competitor's line. Be extra careful at the fence as not everyone will have the same control as you! Jump two or three cross-poles to get your horse straight, then twice over the upright, twice over the parallel. Walk briskly around to keep your horse warm. With four horses to go before you, jump the upright again, then you will be ready to go into the ring.

The cross country

Preparation

With the showjumping over, if you only have around forty minutes before the cross country, this is a useful routine to follow. Take your stirrup leathers up to cross country length, get out of the way of other horses, sharpen your horse up by moving him off your leg for a short, sharp sprint, then walk quite briskly back to your box. Loosen off the girth, put a sheet over his back and get his boots and tack changed for the cross country phase.

Check your list, change your studs, boots, overreach boots, wipe-on event grease if you are using it (use disposable gloves for this!), grab your stick, non-slip gloves, body protector, medical card and holder, hat and silk. Leave everything tidy for your return to the box and ask your helper to put out paper towels, washing water, anti-sweat rug, spanner, scissors and your first aid box (if you leave it handy you hardly ever need it!).

Riding down to the start box.

The cross country collecting ring

Make your way to the practice area, and on arrival declare your number to the starter or their helper, and you'll be told exactly how long you have to go until your round. The starter will do a quick visual check to make sure you are wearing your number bib, have a tagged hat, approved body protector and medical card visible on your arm.

If the event is running one or two class levels that day, you'll see a few different practice fences of various heights, distinguished by their colour numbers – purple for BE80(T), orange for BE90, pink for BE100.

Walk and trot before you start cantering. Canter around the warm-up area with purpose in a large loop, with quite a firm contact. When your horse is warmed up with a soft, swinging back, you are ready to use the practice fence. If you have just showjumped, you don't need to warm your horse up for long, but the important thing is not to over-jump him as he will need his energy for the course ahead.

Try out your coffin canter and power canter; first jump in the middle of the fence and then a couple of times across on a bit of an angle, if the fence is suitable. If all is well, you are ready to run, as you have just practised all you need to go around the course – coffin canter for all the trickier fences, power for the open ones, and jumping near the flag to practise for the skinny fences.

Three horses before you are due to start, do a couple of walk to canter transitions to make sure your horse is listening and is 'in front of your leg'. With two horses to go, ride forward in an active walk and let him see the start box and a horse leaving.

Ensure you jump the correct fence for your class in the cross country warm-up arena.

> ### TOP TIPS **Between the flags**
>
> Keep the red flag to your right and the white to your left and jump between them!

Starting etiquette

There are many ways to leave the start box. Your coach will have advised which way suits you and your horse, but the main thing is to leave with purpose and enjoy your round.

The starter will call you forward from the collecting ring and give you a countdown, for example 'Two minutes' … 'One minute' … 'Thirty seconds'. Listen out carefully to his instructions as you walk around close to him and decide on what count you want to enter the start box. He'll announce 'Fifteen seconds' then 'Ten seconds'. If you are not already in the box, enter quietly and calmly from the side with your horse facing the exit, ready to go. He will then count down '5, 4, 3, 2, 1, go and good luck!'

Following the signal to go, or when the horse's nose crosses the start line, whichever is the earlier, your round time starts. It will stop once your horse's nose passes the finish line timers.

BE80(T) training coach wishing a competitor good luck at the start.

TOP TIPS In the start box

Helper – you can have assistance to hold your horse in the start box.

Time – it is up to you at what count you enter the start box. With a quiet horse, go into the start box on the fifteen or ten seconds count and wait; with an eager horse, it may be better to walk into the box on five seconds.

Starter counting down a competitor. Note the red and green lights, activated by control.

On the course

Once you've started, your progress around the course is monitored by the fence judges, who relay your progress to the controller and commentator so your connections can hear how you are doing.

Concentrate, stick to your line that you walked and, most of all, enjoy it!

If you do run in to problems, listen to the instructions of a steward or fence judge.

Remember to keep the red flag to your right and white to your left!.

TOP TIPS Colour-coded course

Remember, keep the red flag to your right! Jump through the middle of the red and white flags, like a filling in a sandwich!

Purple fence markers – BE80(T)

Orange fence markers – BE90

Pink fence markers – BE100

Red flag waved at you at shoulder height on cross country course means STOP!

Cross country penalties

(BE100 and below)

Elimination

- Failure to start – you have up to two minutes to go once the starter has said go, otherwise you will be eliminated

- If you deliberately leave the start box during the countdown before the starter says go, you will be penalised: penalties may vary depending on level and individual case, but can include elimination

- Refusals – you can have up to four cumulative refusals, or up to three refusals at the same obstacle before you are eliminated

- Second fall of rider – elimination

- Fall of horse – elimination

- Error of course not rectified – elimination

- Omission of boundary flag or obstacle – elimination

Other penalties

- First refusal, circle or run out – 20 penalties

- Second refusal, run out or circle – 40 penalties

- First fall of rider – 65 penalties

- For every second in excess of the optimum time – 0.4 penalty

- *In BE80(T), for every commenced second faster than a speed of 500mpm, 1 time penalty*

The above are only a selection of the Rules. For all current Rules, check the BE Members' Handbook beforehand and take it with you to all events.

You have up to two minutes to leave the start box once the starter says go.

The finish

It is just as important to finish well as it is to start appropriately. When walking the course, take account of where the finish line timers are, as they will vary from one event to another. Many a rider has done a lovely round but has pulled up too early following the final fence and walked through the finish timers, which would incur time penalties.

It's also not good horsemanship or fair on your horse to pull up abruptly or drop his reins as soon as you have jumped the final fence. Your competition ends once you have gone through the finish line, so ride at a consistent speed appropriate to your class to the finish timers, then pull up gradually until you are in walk. (As you will see from the next main section – Aftercare of the Horse – although your *competition* may have finished at this point, your responsibilities will continue.)

After the competition

As you will have seen, it takes an awful lot of time, patience and expense to put on an event. Always be courteous to the stewards and officials. Many are volunteers who have given up their day so you can have a great day of competition with your horse. Say thanks to the organiser, and if you have been lucky enough to be placed, turn up for the prize-giving in plenty of time and thank the sponsors, too. Prizegivings are important to organisers and sponsors, and competitors are requested to be neatly dressed. You will find that many competitors wear their showjumping kit, complete with hat, when accepting their prizes.

Aftercare of your horse

This begins immediately you have finished your cross country and continues as long as is necessary.

Hopefully you will have had an exhilarating but uneventful round. The care of your horse at this stage is of the utmost importance. Jump off your horse's back and loosen off his girth and noseband to give him a well-deserved rest, no matter what the round was like.

Lead your horse at walk back to the lorry and, as you walk, check his shoes, and his freedom of movement. Trot a few strides to check that he's sound. Back at the box, remove his tack, fit his headcollar, remove his studs and boots and wash him down, checking carefully for cuts. When he's been

DIETARY TIPS After the event

In the immediate post-event period you need to have carbohydrates that are absorbed and digested quickly to get glucose into your muscles to replenish glycogen. Postponing carbohydrate consumption after the day's exertions delays muscle glycogen replenishment and can cause tiredness.

Dress smartly in your showjumping kit and hat for the prizegiving, and remember to thank the organiser and sponsor.

washed and the excess water scraped off, put on an anti-sweat rug, offer him a little drink, and walk him around until he is dry. It's imperative that he's kept warm, so his muscles can cool down gradually. Take care of his legs. (See Veterinary Tips.)

Teamwork can help the day go well!

Give him a pick of grass, then put him back in the box. Never leave your horse tied to the outside of your box or trailer on his own and wander off. Someone must always stay with him if he is having his hay outside.

Leave the water available. He shouldn't overdo the drinking if you have kept him hydrated throughout the day. Tie up a haynet and, when his legs are dry and you have double-checked for cuts or bangs, put on his travel boots for the journey home.

EVENT GROOM'S TIPS Cooling down

Cooling down is equally as important as warming up. Know your horse's temperature, pulse and respiratory rate and what his normal range is. Ask your vet to note these down for you and show you how to monitor them. ➤

Don't just pull up your horse after the cross country phase, instead get off, loosen the girth and keep him walking until he has stopped blowing. On hot days remove the saddle and wash him off as soon as possible, removing excess water with a sweat scraper. Repeat if needed – keeping him walking in a shaded area between washing.

If it is cool, ensure that an anti-sweat rug is used after washing.

Dehydration is a great concern for horses doing strenuous work and getting horses to drink 'strange' water can be a problem. Pour about a mug full of pure apple juice into the water bucket to get fussy horses to drink, or alternately 'carrot bobbing' is a great way of encouraging a drink (preferably slice the carrots into thin lengths).

After the cross country phase, wash your horse down as quickly as possible.

Veterinary advice on aftercare

The following offers both ways of checking wellbeing and advice on what to do in the event of a problem.

Correct management of your horse after the cross country will help to maximise his recovery from this phase; thorough assessment will help you spot any potential problems – and thus get any assistance necessary as quickly as possible.

Temperature, pulse and respiration

A horse's normal resting temperature is between 37 and 38 degrees centigrade. After travelling or work the temperature may be above 38 degrees, but should start to fall back to normal resting levels once the travelling or work ceases.

Heat produced by muscle exertion during the cross country will raise your horse's body temperature. After the cross country, unless it is a very hot day, your horse will start to cool off as he walks back to the lorry, where he can be washed off. In hot conditions cool him with iced water, if available,

Every affiliated event has a horse ambulance standing by.

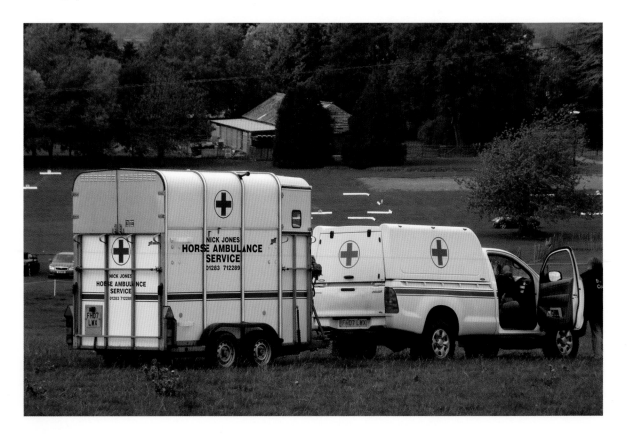

which should then be scraped off, interspersed with short periods of walking, especially if he's blowing hard. The washing, scraping and walking should be repeated until his heart rate, respiratory rate and temperature return towards normal. (It is useful, on a routine home visit from your vet, to get advice on how to monitor and establish these norms for your horse.)

Studs and shoes

It's advisable to remove studs before taking off your boots or bandages. Unnecessary stud-related injuries can happen if the horse kicks out whilst being washed off, or treads on himself whilst being turned in a tight circle. Injuries include lacerations, hock joint and coffin joint penetrations and hoof wall injuries.

If your horse has lost a shoe, the foot should be protected with a boot or bandage if you have to walk over hard or stony ground to get back to the stable or lorry.

Legs

Wash your horse's legs carefully and check thoroughly for any injuries, small nicks, bleeding, heat or swelling.

Cooling the legs helps to reduce heat generated within the flexor tendons during galloping, and to counteract inflammation caused by jarring or trauma. Apply ice or ice packs with tubular bandages, or cold boots, to the areas covering the tendons and fetlock joints and to any specific areas of injury.

Remember, ice or frozen substances should not be placed in direct contact with the skin, so make sure you have a barrier, like a tea towel, in between. Ice should be applied for twenty minutes, and then removed for at least twenty to thirty minutes. Cold therapy will reduce swelling and have an analgesic effect; therefore legs should be examined later for any signs of injury that may have been masked. (Cold therapy causes vasoconstriction followed by deep tissue vasodilatation and promotes an increase in circulatory flow.) Many leg-cooling machines and boots are available, although some may not be as effective as using ice.

Legs should be carefully dried afterwards to prevent skin irritation then clay can be smoothed on once cold therapy is finished – inspect legs again first and don't apply clay over small abrasions or cuts.

Following a one-day event, trot your horse up when you get home and check his legs, then do the same again the following day before any further work.

If you suspect a soft tissue injury, like a tendon or ligament strain, it's important to take your vet's advice on how to manage the injury in the initial stages, and the appropriate time for the injury to be scanned. The degree of lameness and inflammation is not always a true reflection on the severity of the injury. Initially cold therapy like ice, cold hosing, or cold water hydrotherapy and rest are important. Correctly applied bandages may provide support but it's important to remember that incorrectly applied or over-tightened bandages can do more harm than good.

Wound management

Examine any wounds, however small, carefully. Assess the extent of the wound, its proximity to any joints or tendon sheath and check for any leakage of synovial fluid. If in any doubt, get in contact with the duty vet. Certainly consult them if the wound is bleeding excessively, is accompanied by lameness, or if it's close to a joint or tendon sheath. Very small wounds over the knees can penetrate joints or the extensor tendon sheaths, likewise joint penetration can occur from wounds around the fetlocks, hocks or stifles, or stud wounds around the coronary band. Overreach wounds in the pastern region can penetrate the flexor tendon sheath.

Scrapes over stifles are common eventing injuries. They can be iced, but any excessive lameness or swelling may indicate a more serious problem, such as a fractured patella, so shouldn't be ignored.

Wounds must be cleaned thoroughly to remove dirt and any foreign material and to reduce the risk of infection. Excessive bleeding can be controlled by applying pressure in the form of a bandage with padding, or direct pressure on the wound until the vet arrives. Once cleaned, minor wounds can be dressed and bandaged.

In the event of any excessive lameness or a suspected fracture, call the event vet. Meanwhile keep the horse still and follow their advice over the phone or event radio until they get to you.

Tying-up

If your horse 'ties-up' at an event, the signs may range from a shortening of his stride length and vague stiffness, to complete 'setfast', sweating and colic signs. Stop riding and call the event vet straight away. Don't be tempted to carry on riding as this can cause further muscle damage. Horses can 'tie-up' at any stage at an event, but most commonly when warming up for dressage or on the cross country.

Back at the yard

On arrival home, trot your horse a few strides to check that he is OK, then get him settled for the night as quickly as possible with his feed, with salts added if you haven't been able to give him any electrolytes or salts earlier, to help replace those lost in sweating at the competition. Check him quietly again last thing.

Leave all your tack stripped and washed and put anything to be repaired out to one side. Muck out your lorry or trailer. Never leave it wet and soiled, or before you know it you will be renewing the floor.

Check the ground around and under your trailer or box before you leave to make sure you have all your kit.

EVENT GROOM'S TIPS **Care of tack**

To clean really mucky tack covered in mud or grease get some warm water with a little washing-up liquid and use a scouring sponge. The scourer is strong enough to remove any caked-on dirt without damaging the leather. Then use a good leather balsam to keep the leather supple and soft.

11

WHO'S WHO
AT AFFILIATED EVENTS

When you're at an event it's helpful to know who does what and where, so that, if you need it, you can get help.

BE officials

BE employs regional coordinators who cover events from Scotland to the South West of England. It also employs training officers, who run the accredited coaches scheme and training for members and officials. It does not employ the organisers – they run their own events with support and guidance from BE. For example the training officer, scorer and regional co-ordinator are all employed by BE, whilst the steward is a volunteer who acts as an independent monitor and, if needed, an adjudicator.

Regional coordinator (RC)

A regional coordinator works part-time for BE and is their 'eyes and ears' on the ground. RCs liaise with existing organisers and help them in the planning and running of their event to help make it as successful as possible. They also identify new sites and meet potential organisers who want to start up an affiliated event, and arrange training for officials and fence judges in their area. They are a great source of advice and help for BE members. Their contact details can be found in *British Eventing Life* Magazine or under your local region on the BE website.

The tools of the trade –
an official's lot, complete
with coffee!

Technical adviser (TA)

The technical adviser works part-time for BE and covers a range of different events around the country. The TA is responsible for all technical aspects of the event, and makes a site visit to an upcoming event to measure the cross country course to ensure that it is built within BE guidelines and standards for that level. The TA also chooses the rider representative (see later) in consultation with the organiser.

On the day of the event the TA works with the organising team to ensure that the event runs smoothly. Duties include checking the going, walking and agreeing the showjumping course with the course builder and liaising with the fence repair team on the cross country course. At the start of the day, the TA briefs the fence judges on their duties and assists and supports the steward in his duties on the day.

Scorer

The scorer helps prepare the timetable in advance of events, along with the secretary and organiser, and manages the scheduling of competitors who are riding several horses, known as multiple riders. On the day, the scorer is

A scorer at work.

in charge of volunteer scorers, provisional scorers, scoreboard writers and runners. The scorers' office is a pretty busy place, as all scores for all riders from all three phases pass through their office!

Event officials

Organiser

The organiser is the landowner or tenant who puts on and runs the event. He is responsible for employing a cross country course designer and builder, showjumping and dressage officials, and getting the event ready to run on time. He also has the huge task of organising upwards of 150 volunteers for each day of his event – no mean feat! On the day he deals with queries from competitors, owners and trainers. If the queries are of a technical nature, or involve the interpretation of BE Rules and Regulations, they are referred to the steward, technical adviser or regional coordinator.

Event secretary

The event secretary (and their team of helpers) is usually the first official you will locate on arrival at an event in order to collect your number, pay your start fee and show your horse's passport and vaccination record. You can also get your hat tagged at the secretary's if it is your first event or you have bought a new hat.

They are a great source of information for the whole event and you can also locate other personnel from their office as the secretary can put out a call for them over the radio.

Cross country course designer and builder

The course designer and builder is sometimes the same person, but more often than not the course designer is freelance and will work with a team of freelance course builders.

To design and build BE courses, they have to be accredited and must design and build to BE standards. Designers are rated from A to C, with the more experienced designers on List A. Builders are rated from platinum to bronze, depending on what courses and at what level they build.

On the day of your event, the course builders double as the fence repair team and will be on hand for emergency repairs or course changes.

Steward

At an event, what the steward says, goes! He is in overall charge of the event and, on the day, he is the person who allows the phases to start once all the pre-course checks have been made. His go-to person on the day is usually the TA or the organiser. The steward ensures that the competition is run in accordance with the rules and is responsible for any disciplinary matters. The steward is a trained volunteer – not employed by BE – and is completely neutral. Other duties of the steward include pre-event checks, usually with

OPPOSITE A TA checking the height of a fence.

The steward keeping a watchful eye as the first competition starts in the showjump arena.

the organiser and TA to ensure that all is going to plan in the build-up and preparation for the event.

The steward will adjudicate on any unforeseen eventualities, settling any protest or objection.

Control

Control is the lynchpin of an event, and thus can be found in a prominent place on the cross country course, usually in an elevated viewing box that you will see when you walk around the course. The control team consists of the commentator, controller(s), plotter and provisional scorer. When a horse is just about to start, the starter or one of his team call through to the plotter in control to let them know which competitor is about to set out on the course, so the commentator can start his commentary and control can then monitor that round. Control can also operate a stop/go or red/green light facility that is connected to the start, thus dictating whether a horse can go or not. This will be only be used if there is a problem ahead on the course and they need to delay the next horse to start.

An event runs two or more radio networks, depending on its size and the number of classes. For example the fence judges will be on the same network as the commentator, which is called Fence Net. Officials or Emergency

Net is the name of the other network, connecting the TA, steward, vet(s), doctor(s), paramedic, horse ambulance, fence repair, starter, organiser and secretary. The controller listens to two networks at once via a pair of headphones, with Fence Net in one ear and Officials Net in the other. It takes a great deal of skill to monitor all communication and react when necessary. The controller and commentator sit side-by-side and in front of them is a plot board, which charts the progress of a rider around the course. The board has each fence numbered and named, and whenever a new horse starts, one of the stewards in control clips the printout of the competitor's details, such as dressage and showjumping score (plus the bit of commentator's information you write about yourself and your horse when you make an entry) to a plot peg, and this is moved along the board as each fence judge relays information to the controller, for example, 'Competitor number 246 clear at fence eight.'

Starter

There can be up to six people in a start and finish team: in addition to the starter, a chief time keeper, a finish time keeper, a recorder and one or more collecting ring stewards.

The starter or his assistant will check that you have essentials on you like your hat, body protector and medical card. Once you have declared your number, he will let you know when you are a minute or so off your time, and will count you down from there. He is responsible for recording your time around the course, from start to finish. Horses are usually started at two-minute intervals. At some of the bigger competitions, you will find that competitors are started at one-and-a-half minute intervals. On average two hundred horses and riders will pass through the cross country start on any one competition day.

Event volunteers

Events rely on a small army of volunteers who all mobilise for the day of your event! On an average day, running one or two levels of competition, an event will rely on over 150 volunteers. If an organiser is running two or three days of competition, that will be upwards of 400 volunteers over the three days. Please remember to say 'thank you' when you can!

Dressage and showjump judges

A dressage judge will only judge one section in a class, but with around 42 competitors in a section, this can take half a day to work through. Dressage judges are qualified to judge following training with British Dressage (BD).

Dressage judges are accompanied by writers, who sit with the judges and write down the judge's marks and comments on an individual's dressage test sheet. Nimble fingers are required for this job.

The showjump judge on the day is very often the showjumping course designer and builder, who is joined by a commentator and scorer plus the main arena party, who are responsible for putting up the fences when poles are knocked down. The showjump judge is trained to design and build courses by British Showjumping (BS).

The showjump course builder altering the course.

Fence judges

There will be two fence judges for each cross country obstacle. If a couple of fences are close together, a pair of fence judges may look after two fences and chart a competitor's progress over both. Their essentials are a timing watch, a whistle to alert spectators of approaching horses and a carbon copy log book and pen. They also have a radio tuned in to Cross Country Net and a set of emergency flags. Fence judges are asked by the TA at the morning briefing to pick out a timing landmark some way before their fence. Every horse is timed going past the timing landmark, the reading is entered into the log book by the fence judge and a second reading is entered once the horse has jumped the fence. This is so that, in the eventuality of a hold-up on course, fence judges can safely stop an approaching combination once they have passed their timing landmark and have an accurate time reading to put in the log book. Once the course has reopened and the stopped combination has a chance to warm up again, the fence judges will take another reading when the combination has passed their timing landmark. The timing watch does not act like a stopwatch. All timing equipment is synchronised, so as soon as the button is depressed, it is recorded, so all fence judges, starter and control have the same event time.

Collecting ring stewards

Stewards are responsible for the smooth running of the collecting ring, whether it is for the showjumping or dressage arena. The number of stewards depends on how big an event is and how many rings and sections are running. An average BE80(T), BE90 or BE100 event will have one showjumping arena and four dressage arenas. The remit of the stewards is to mark off your number once you have declared, make a quick visual check of your tack, and let you know if the arena is running to time and how many riders are to go before you.

Score collectors (runners and scoreboard writers)

The runners continuously make their rounds and take completed dressage test sheets and copies of the log book records from the showjumping stewards and individual fence judges on the cross country course to the scorer's tent. They can usually be spotted on a quad bike or motorbike with a bag

Fence judges and the
score collector at work.

full of papers. At some of the large events, runners are only needed on the
cross country section because scores are entered electronically into the
scoreboard database at the dressage and showjumping arena. The scoreboard
writers' job is to go between the scorers and the results boards and write in
the latest individual's penalties on the big sheets fixed to the results boards.

Rider representative

The rider representative is chosen by the TA or organiser a few days before
the event. They usually choose a professional rider who is experienced
at riding at different levels. If this person agrees, then they must be available for queries on that day. If the event is quite large and runs over several
days, or that rider is competing on several horses, then more than one rider
representative may be chosen. Their name and telephone number can be
found pinned up in the secretary's tent.

The role of the rider representative is an important one, and it is to listen to the concerns of other riders. They can be asked any number of queries on the day, from 'How do I ride that drop fence', to ' I think that skinny fence needs to have a tree on the left to stop horses from running out', or 'I think the ground is too deep in the showjumping, can some of the fences be moved?' It is the role of the rider representative to consider all queries, answer them if they can and, if not, to get back to the competitor with an answer after speaking to the relevant party, whether it be the steward, TA, secretary or organiser.

British Eventing training days

British Eventing offer training days for those involved behind the scenes at events, visit www.britisheventing.com/training to find courses in your region.

12

A SAFER SPORT

Safety is paramount in eventing, in recognition that it's a risk sport. Here you'll find details of advances on the cross country including the safety research fence. You'll also learn about the veterinary and medical provisions on an affiliated course, plus essential equipment standards for you and your transport.

Safety advances

British Eventing is constantly working towards managing risk to provide the safest courses for horses and riders whilst retaining the integrity and thrill of the sport. At the end of last century, BE and the FEI carried out a complete review of safety and risk management. A committee was formed under the chairmanship of Lord Hartington to look at safety in the sport and recommend changes.

Recommendations from the Hartington Enquiry have been rolled out, including the fall report form. Completed by fence judges and entered into the BE database by TAs, it monitors every fence jumped on a BE affiliated event in Britain, which can then be analysed mid-season to address any concerns.

Research and development

BE has pioneered many safety advances, including a programme of research with the Transport Research Laboratory (TRL), perhaps more commonly known for their crash test dummy work with car manufacturers to establish

The Safety Research fence in action. Note the camera to the left of the photo.

vehicle safety standards. Following that force and resistance testing, frangible (collapsing) fences were conceived, with the introduction of frangible pins, which can now be seen at events all over the world. These allow a rail to drop away if a horse breasts it, to help avoid a somersault fall. Work is also ongoing on the development of the second-generation pin, and also the reverse pinning method used on fences where traditional pinning wouldn't be suitable.

BE have also implemented a fence description form which describes the approach, landing, fence design, dimension and profile for every obstacle jumped, which is analysed mid-season, along with the fall report data.

BE has also worked with safety leaders such as Goodyear and engineers at Bristol University to build the safety research fence, which is equipped with a camera to film critical data and fitted with special load cells which record the forces exerted when a horse hits a fence. This, in turn, has helped to determine possible causes of rotational falls and is an example of where technical engineering has influenced course design for the benefit of horse and rider.

Course design and construction

Course design and construction continues to evolve as new ideas come forward. BE has guidelines for course designers and builders which are constantly reviewed and updated. These guidelines set the framework for designers and builders and should be used in conjunction with the up-to-date rules and regulations regarding permitted fence dimensions.

All course builders and designers have to undergo thorough training before being certified as approved, and are required to build and design at entry level with an experienced team before being permitted to design or build at higher levels.

Health and safety considerations for the site

As well as physical improvements to the cross country course, other safety factors are taken into account for the site as a whole and organisers must appoint a qualified health and safety steward to approve the site well before the event starts. This official looks at provisions for traffic control, access points, routes for emergency vehicles, horse-walks, spectator areas and much more.

As mentioned earlier, organisers also appoint volunteer rider representatives, who are there competing on the day and whose name and telephone

Signage on a horse-walk at a busy crossing point.

number are available for fellow competitors to call if they are concerned about safety, or issues about the course.

Riders are also restricted to five cross country rides in any one day of competition.

Medical and veterinary provision

Doctors and fully-equipped ambulances are mandatory for all affiliated events, and they will be on site at various points of the cross country course when it is running and at key areas around the event. It is likely that there will be at least two event doctors plus paramedics at any one event.

For your horse's safety, an equine vet will be present, unless it is purely a dressage day. (Some events offer the option to do your dressage the day before the jumping phases, if they know they will be heavily subscribed.) The number of event vets on site usually depends on the size of the event and the number of classes. There must also be a fully manned horse ambulance.

Procedure following fall of rider

If you fall in the showjumping or cross country phase, you will need to be cleared by the event doctor before you get on again or ride any other horses. If you take a tumble in the dressage, the BE steward can clear you to ride

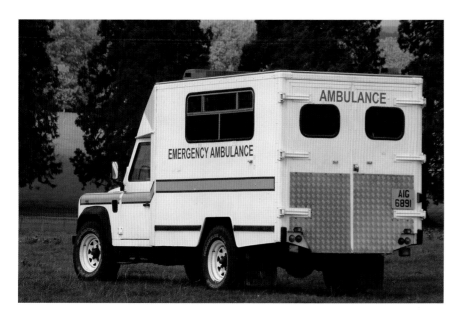

Fully-equipped ambulances, ideally capable of going off road, are mandatory at all events.

after consultation with ambulance personnel. If, following a fall, you need medical assistance, you may receive a medical suspension for a set number of days before you can compete again. There are minimum suspension periods following head or neck injuries.

It's imperative that you have filled in your details on your BE medical card and take it with you to every event. You cannot ride if you don't have

Following a fall, you may be required to report to the event doctor.

it clearly visible on your arm for the cross country phase. Many body protectors have a plastic sleeve attached to the shoulder protector for this very purpose.

When you return to competition following a medical suspension, your medical card must be signed by the event doctor before you continue, or else you could be disciplined. The event doctor can also request random dope testing and medical spot checks on riders.

Procedure following fall of horse

If your horse falls at a practice fence, you cannot continue until he's cleared by the event vet. Once cleared, you can then liaise with the steward about a revised start time. Your horse is deemed to have fallen when both his shoulder and quarters have touched either the ground, or the obstacle and the ground simultaneously. For more details on penalties, see pages 180 and 187.

Protective equipment for eventing

Headgear

All hats for eventing in BE80(T) to BE100 Plus classes must conform to a minimum European Standard, which will have an EN or BSEN prefix followed by a number, or a PAS prefix, again followed by a number. It must also have the British Standard Institute (BS) Kitemark or the SEI (Safety Equipment Institute of America) symbol. (It's imperative to check the BE *Members' Handbook* for the latest protective headwear regulation for the sport, as Standards are constantly reviewed to reflect advances in headgear protection.)

When you are about to purchase a new hat, be aware that many countries have different standards, so even though the hat may bear, for example, the EN1384 Standard, it may be prefixed by other initials belonging to the country testing the helmet (for example DIN EN1384 shows it was tested in Germany), and so could not be worn eventing in the UK.

The BS prefix symbolises that the hat has been tested in Britain and while, in theory, there should be no difference, some European countries have approved helmets that may have failed if tested in Britain. So, for BE competitions, make sure yours has the BS prefix.

Correct headgear must be worn for all phases.

When riding at an event, whether in the horsebox park or between phases, approved hats must be worn at all times, with the integral adjustable harness fitted correctly.

Body protectors

Designed to absorb impact from a fall or a kick from a horse, body protectors are compulsory for the cross country phase of eventing. Make sure you buy a British Equestrian Trade Association (BETA) Approved Standard body protector and have it fitted by a qualified fitter as, importantly for eventing, it shouldn't impair your flexibility or balance.

The BETA Standard sets criteria for shock-absorption, controls the area of the body that must be covered and ensures that there are minimal gaps between the protective foam panels. It encompasses three levels, each designed for different activities and denoted by a colour-coded label on the garment.

You must have a Level 3 body protector for eventing, with the current mandatory year Standard on the label, which is located clearly on the outside for ease of inspection when at an event. Check the BE *Members' Handbook* for the current Level and Standard required. For the most up to date product information and advice visit the safety pages on www.beta-uk.org.

Most body protectors are made from heat-sensitive foam, so they'll feel increasingly comfortable as they soften and mould to your body. Store your protector in a warm (but not artificially hot) place to ensure that it's nice and flexible for your cross country round.

If you choose to wear an air jacket, you must wear it over the top of your BETA-approved body protector, unless it is a BETA-approved, combined version of an air jacket and body protector. If you fall on course and your air jacket inflates but you want to continue, you must remove your air

An inflatable air jacket – unless it is the integral type – must be worn over a level 3 body protector, with the medical armband clearly visible.

Think about replacing your body protector every three to five years, unless you have a bad fall and damage is evident.

jacket. If it is a combined jacket, you can continue once you have removed the cannister, which deflates the air jacket.

Following a fall

Generally, think about replacing your body protector every three to five years as the impact absorption properties of the foam may decline.

After a fall, check your body protector for dents. The foam will expand back to its original shape within thirty minutes, but if a dent is evident, then it's likely that this part of the protector has lost its impact absorption properties and should be replaced. Some manufacturers sell replacement panels, so if you body protector is fairly new it may be worth making a call to ask.

Shoulder protectors

Research into eventing falls has shown that wearing BETA Level 3 shoulder protectors can reduce the risk of breaking a collarbone by up to 80 per cent. Once fitted to your body protector you don't have to re-fit them every time you ride, but they can easily be replaced if damaged as they are usually fitted with Velcro.

> **TOP TIPS Getting the right fit**
>
> - Wear the body protector for about five minutes in the warmth to let the heat of your body soften the foam and allow it to mould to the contours of your body.
>
> - It should fit securely and reasonably tightly to avoid movement during activity and to stay in place in the event of an accident
>
> - Practise your forward and jumping seat, also leaning back during a drop and your sitting deep position for comfort and fit while on a saddle horse.
>
> - The top of the body protector should just reach the top of your breastbone at the front and the prominent bone at the base of the back of your neck.
>
> - The front of the body protector should be not less than 25mm below the ribcage.
>
> - The body protector must fit all the way round your torso.
>
> - The body protector and shoulder protector should cover the whole collarbone between them.
>
> - The bottom of the back of the body protector should not touch the saddle when mounted, so try the protector sitting on the saddle horse in the shop. (Some manufacturers offer a short version or a shortening service.)

Transport issues

Legal to drive?

It is advisable to check the DVLA or VOSA (www.vosa.gov.uk/Guide-for-Horsebox-Owners) websites for up-to-date guidance, but basically if you passed your driving test for a car on or after 1 January 1997, you can only drive vehicles with a maximum authorised mass of up to 3.5 tonnes. If your horsebox or vehicle and trailer exceed 3.5 tonnes, you must apply for the provisional entitlement for one of the following categories and in turn take the necessary test:

- Category C1 covers vehicles up to 7.5 tonnes.

- Category C covers vehicles of any size.

Most horse trailer and towing vehicle combinations exceed 3,500kg, as most four-wheel drive towing vehicles exceed 3,500kg.

If you passed your driving test before 1 January 1997, you are entitled to drive vehicles up to 7.5 tonnes with a trailer. The combination weight must not exceed 8.25 tonnes. This is covered by category C1+E. This entitlement would usually remain valid until the day before the driver's seventieth birthday. If the driver wishes to renew the entitlement, they would need to complete a D2 application form and have a D4 medical form completed by their doctor.

Make sure you are legal to drive.

Towing capacity

To find out if you can tow a trailer with your car, have a look in the vehicle handbook and also on the chassis plate, usually located under the bonnet, as every vehicle manufacturer has to give a maximum towing weight. As a basic guide, the unladen weight of the trailer, plus the weight of the heaviest horses to be towed, must not exceed the trailer's maximum authorised mass. This, in turn, should not exceed the car's maximum towing weight.

As a rule, the gross weight of the trailer should not exceed 80 per cent of the gross weight of the car. Not many ordinary cars can comfortably tow a loaded trailer, even if they are legally entitled to do so, because the brakes and suspension are not built to cope with such a strain. It is far better to tow with a four-wheel drive vehicle and you will find things like braking, pulling off and manoeuvring are much easier, as well as creating a more comfortable ride for your horse.

TOP TIPS Towing

- Ensure that you have a roadside recovery service for you and your horse should you break down away from home.

- Towing speed limits are 30mph on a road with street lighting, 50mph on a dual carriageway and 60mph on a motorway.

- Before you drive away from the yard, check that all lights work, tyres are the correct pressure and you have a useable spare.

- Check the tow bar is securely on, level and at the right height.

- Ensure you have attached the breakaway cable to the car.

- Get your trailer serviced annually.

- Check the floor every time before you travel by lifting any matting and prodding the flooring.

For the latest advice, which includes information on the use of tachographs and driving for reward, pick up a copy of the VOSA publication, *A Guide for Horsebox and Trailer Owners*.

INDEX